CREATIVE INTERVENTIONS
WORKBOOK

PRACTICAL TOOLS TO STOP INTERPERSONAL VIOLENCE

**Welcome to the *Creative Interventions Workbook:*
*Practical Tools to Stop Interpersonal Violence.***

All content is the same as the Workbook available on www.creative-interventions.org.

This workbook is a companion version to the more extensive *Creative Interventions Toolkit*, also published in paperback by AK Press and available for free pdf download in English and Spanish at www.creative-interventions.org/toolkit.

© 2022 Creative Interventions

Permission to reproduce and adapt all content with acknowledgment of Creative Interventions. Take this work, use it and make it your own!

HOW ARE YOU USING THIS WORKBOOK?
PLEASE SHARE YOUR EXPERIENCES

As more people continue to use the Toolkit and Workbook, we are hearing more stories about challenges – and successes – in ending and preventing violence.

Please share your stories on www.creative-interventions.org/stories

We invite you to share your:

- Suggestions for changes or future tools
- Stories about how you were able to use the Toolkit or Workbook for study, organizing, or confronting and transforming violence.

ISBN 978-1-84935-466-0

AK Press
370 Ryan Avenue #100
Chico, CA 95973
USA
www.akpress.org
akpress@akpress.org

AK Press
33 Tower Street
Edinburgh, EH6, 7BN
Scotland
www.akuk.com
akuk@akpress.org

Please contact us to request the latest AK Press distribution catalog, which features books, pamphlets, zines, and stylish apparel published and/or distributed by AK Press. Alternatively, visit our websites for the complete catalog, latest news, and secure ordering.

Cover illustration by Kill Joy (https://justseeds.org/artist/killjoy)
Printed in Canada on acid-free paper

CREATIVE INTERVENTIONS
WORKBOOK

PRACTICAL TOOLS TO STOP INTERPERSONAL VIOLENCE

Table of Contents

✱ PREFACE

WELCOME

This is the **Creative Interventions Workbook: Practical Tools to Stop Interpersonal Violence.**

This workbook is a companion version to the more extensive *Creative Interventions Toolkit*, also published in paperback by AK Press and available for free pdf download in English and Spanish at www.creative-interventions.org/toolkit. There's also an online interactive, Maori/English version created by a Maori group in Aotearoa (New Zealand) at www.mataora.wananga.com.

Creative Interventions started in 2004 in Oakland, CA as a resource center to create community-based interventions to interpersonal violence – domestic violence, intimate partner violence, sexual abuse or assault, or family violence, and other situations of violence in which people know each other. We were interested in creating models and tools to help everyday people address and end violence – by turning to each other – not the police, not systems, not even professional services. We called these community-based interventions. They are now widely known as community accountability or transformative justice – or, simply, creative interventions.

After experimenting with a lot of very different situations of harm and violence, we put everything we learned in the *Creative Interventions Toolkit*. We ended by sharing our model and tools with anyone facing interpersonal violence – or for groups wanting to get together to form a response to violence in their communities.

About This Workbook

The Creative Interventions Workbook is a result of requests for a shorter, more user-friendly version of the *Creative Interventions Toolkit*. It is not a replacement for the more comprehensive toolkit, but a companion.

We encourage you to become familiar with the *Creative Interventions Toolkit* before using the Workbook or while using the workbook. We have included some references to related sections of the Toolkit in order to make this easier. The Creative Interventions website will keep you informed of any language updates of the toolkit or workbook.

We also encourage you to look at other resources – other websites, books, tools, and webinars. To start, you can refer to the resources section at the end of this workbook.

This workbook contains:

Condensed Content: Shorter versions of key pieces from the *Creative Interventions Toolkit*.

Updates: Some new information based upon things we have learned since we published the *Creative Interventions Toolkit* (first made available in 2012).

Adaptable Worksheets: This includes worksheets you'll find in this book and that are available in Google doc or Word doc form at www.creative-interventions.org, so you can make changes to adapt to your situation. The worksheets are for survivors, allies, and people who caused harm – to reflect, prepare, and move toward change.

Resources for Individual and/or Collective/Group Work: Support aimed at both individual and collective work. For example, many of the worksheets come in individual (*my* worksheet) and collective (*our* worksheet) forms, assisting those closest to the harm to work collectively to find solutions to that harm.

How to Use This Workbook

Open source. We welcome you to make a copy, print, download, and share with others. **You do not need our permission.** You can adapt and change the tools according to your needs. Visit our website (www.creative-interventions.org) for downloadable versions – and be sure to read the section on "Internet Security" when you do.

Access. We encourage those of you who are able to read and understand this workbook to support access due to language, visual, literacy, and other access issues. If you make audio or visual recordings or create other accessible tools, please share them with others by sending your ideas to info@creative-interventions.org. We will also work on making other accessible versions available on our website as they become available.

Give us feedback. Share your stories.

If you find this document useful, please consider sharing a story about how you used these resources or telling us more about your experience at www.creative-interventions.org/stories. You can also sign up for the Creative Interventions email list on our website or follow CI on Facebook.

Acknowledgments

Special thanks to Sid Jordan for project consulting and content management, Mimi Kim for adaptation and updates, and Audrey Kuo for extensive edits. We give our deep gratitude to the many co-collaborators and comrades who worked as workbook reviewers:

DeAnn Alcantara-Thompson
Angeli Bhatt
Rachel Caidor
Tara Cantu-Nishimoto
Megyung Chung
Andy Coco
Kiyomi Fujikawa
Yessica Gonzalez
Donna Harati
Rachel Herzing
Tamaso Johnson
Martina Kartman
Audrey Kuo
RJ Maccani
Chelsea Miller
Mia Mingus
Soniya Munshi
Claudia Peña
Mariella Saba
daNaE TaPiA

Thanks again to the Creative Interventions team that originally created the *Creative Interventions Toolkit* upon which this workbook is based: Sutapa Balaji, Leo Bruenn, Juan Cuba, Rachel Herzing, Mimi Kim, Isabel Kang, Isaac Ontiveros, and Orchid Pusey. Special thanks to Kalei Kanuha for your guidance and evaluation.

 ABOUT
CREATIVE
INTERVENTIONS

WHAT DO WE BELIEVE?

Creative Interventions was first created as a resource center to create models and tools that could be used to reduce, end, and prevent interpersonal violence. Interpersonal violence includes domestic violence, intimate partner violence, sexual abuse or assault, family violence, and other situations of violence in which people know each other.

We know that survivors or victims of violence usually first turn to the people they know for support rather than hotlines, advocates, or the police. Family and friends are usually the "first responders," but don't always know what to do. Some of us have nowhere else to go for help – no crisis lines, advocates, or shelters available, or none that understand us and our situation. Many of us are unwilling or unable to go to the police.

The purpose of this workbook is to bring knowledge and skills back to communities and support those closest to violence to reduce, end, and prevent it.

Interpersonal violence often involves people we care about, including the person who caused harm. Responding to these kinds of harm can be difficult. We may not want to recognize that those close to us may also be the ones harming us. We may fear losing someone close to us. We may fear that coming forward will cause unwanted consequences to the person causing harm – or to ourselves. We may also fear that they will wind up in jail, that immigration authorities might take them away, that they might lose their job, or that others will look down on us or our family.

Creative Interventions builds on the belief that interventions to interpersonal violence are the most meaningful and effective if they come from those closest to and most impacted by the violence. The people most affected are typically the ones who also know the most about the people involved in violence, who understand the culture and resources of the community in which violence is happening, and who ultimately have the most to lose from violence and the most to gain from ending it.

This is why we first called these "community-based interventions to violence." Some people now know this approach as community accountability or transformative justice.

OUR MODEL AT A GLANCE

The Creative Interventions Model is an approach to violence or harm intervention that asks a set of questions. These questions can be useful whether you are in a state of rapid response to a crisis – or involved in a more step-by-step process that might move toward a resolution to harm and change and transformation for everyone affected by that violence (see more about some of the differences between rapid response and a process on page 27).

Together these areas for reflection and decision-making make up what we call our **Tools to Mix and Match**:

> **A. Getting Clear.** What Is Going On?
>
> **B. Staying Safe.** How Do We Stay Safe?
>
> **C. Mapping Allies and Barriers.** Who Can Help?
>
> **D. Setting Goals.** What Do We Want?
>
> **E. Supporting Survivors or Victims.** How Can We Help?
>
> **F. Taking Accountability.** How Do We Change Violence?
>
> **G. Working Together.** How Do We Work Together as a Team?
>
> **H. Keeping on Track.** How Do We Move Forward?

On the following pages, you will find versions of **Tools to Mix and Match:**

Philly Stands Up created a simple single-page worksheet (back and front) visual of each of these tools and key questions you can ask.

Creative Interventions made a comprehensive matrix or grid meant to be pictured side-by-side to imagine where you are in your intervention – and some useful questions at that stage.

The Creative Interventions Model by Philly Stands Up

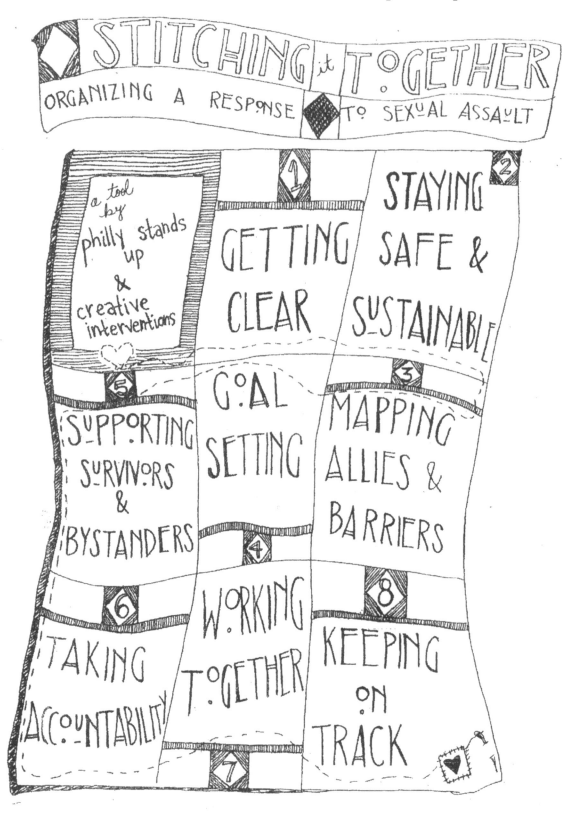

The Creative Interventions Model by Philly Stands Up

/////////// **QUESTIONS TO CONSIDER WHEN ORGANIZING A RESPONSE TO SEXUAL ASSAULT** ///////////	**Getting Clear:** • What is going on? • What kind of violence or abuse has happened or is happening? • Who is getting harmed? • Who is doing the harming?	**Staying safe and sustainable:** • What are risks and dangers right now? • Risks to whom? What level of risk? • What are the risks & dangers if we take no action? • What are the risks & dangers if we take action? • Who needs safety & protection? • What plans can we make to provide safety & protection? • What do we need to do for self and community care? • Where are we vulnerable to burnout?

Supporting survivors/ bystanders: • What violence or abuse did the survivor experience? • What harms have resulted? • What do they think will be helpful to them? • Who can best offer this support? • How are they getting ongoing support? • How are you taking care of yourself to provide that support?	**Goal setting:** • What do you want? • What do you not want? • What would you consider a success?	**Mapping allies and barriers:** • Who can help? • Who can get in the way? • Who is in a good position to support the survivor? • Who is in a good position to offer support to the person or people doing harm? • Who can become an ally or become a better ally with a little bit of help? • What kind of help do they need and who can give it? • How can you draw on resources offered by organizations?

Taking accountability: • What concrete interventions could make the violence stop? • What could prevent further violence? • What are the points of leverage? How can they be used? • What milestones do you hope to reach? • What reparations are needed to promote survivor and community safety & healing?	**Working together:** • Who has the capacity to work on the process? • Is everybody prepared to use a harm-reduction model & meet people where they're at? • What identities & skills would be strategic to have on the team? • Does everyone know & agree with the goals? • How will you resolve disagreements? • What are their roles? • How will you communicate & coordinate? • How will you make decisions?	**Keeping on track:** • Are we ready to take the next step? • How did it go? • What did we achieve? • Did we celebrate our achievements (even the small ones)? • What needs to change? • What is the next step?

OUR APPROACH TO INTERVENTIONS

What Do We Mean by an Intervention?

The word *intervention* is about taking action. It means that there is something we can do about violence – whether it was in the past, is happening now, or might happen in the future. Interventions are rarely one-time events, but are usually a set of actions that different people can take, playing different roles, and that are better done if coordinated together. You might call what you do other things: circles, processes, rapid response.

What Are Community-Based Interventions to Violence?

We at Creative Interventions call our interventions **community-based interventions** or **community-based responses to violence**. The word community acknowledges that it is not only individuals but also communities that are harmed when violence occurs. It tells us that interpersonal violence is not only an individual problem, but a community problem. It also tells us that communities can be the very place where we find the best and longest-lasting solutions to violence.

> We usually think of the person who caused harm as the one to be accountable for violence. *Community accountability* also means that communities are accountable for often ignoring, minimizing, or even encouraging violence. Communities must also recognize, end, and take responsibility for violence by becoming more knowledgeable, skillful, and willing to take action to intervene in violence. The community is where we can create a culture and conditions that prevent violence from happening in the first place.

What Is Community Accountability?

We also call our approach to intervention ***community accountability*** because it is the community that has the responsibility and the power to end violence. The community can create a culture and norms where people who cause harm know that they must take responsibility or accountability for that harm – and where everybody can deeply understand and practice accountability. The word accountability is the ability to recognize, end, and take responsibility for violence – and ultimately to repair the harm and take action to make sure that it does not happen again.

What Is Transformative Justice?

These responses to violence are also part of the concept we know as ***transformative justice*** – based in social justice, not in police and prisons or the criminal legal system. Transformative justice is not only a way of approaching violence – it is a belief system or even a way of life in which:

1. We understand that **violence is rooted in systemic inequality and injustice** such as racism, sexism, ableism, and poverty; that homophobia and transphobia form the foundations for violence; that discrimination against immigrants and certain religions or national origins create the conditions for violence;

2. We believe that solutions to violence **should not cause further violence** – therefore, we will not use the police to solve interpersonal violence – nor will we use street justice or vigilante violence to end violence;

3. We believe that we can use **compassion, care, and connection** to confront and transform violence – rather than revenge and punishment – even for serious harms; and

4. We believe that **anyone can be transformed** toward change. What we as a society may lack are the values, skills, and capacity to create a world where transformative justice is fully supported and given all the resources it needs.

This workbook is one small step in addressing these needs.

Is this restorative justice?

Restorative justice has many similarities to the work of Creative Interventions – and has been an inspiration for much of our work. Restorative justice has also come to mean many, many different things. Some practices are similar to or even the same as some of the community accountability or transformative justice processes we do. But much of restorative justice has also become very professionalized – taking place with experts, many times working with the police or prosecutors or courts – and taken out of the context of its Indigenous or First Nation roots. While these forms of restorative justice may, in some cases, provide better options than the usual punitive systems, they are still very often tied to the police and to law enforcement. They may only be available to those already arrested and/or incarcerated. Because of this common trend in restorative justice, we are careful in using this term and ask for thoughtfulness in choosing the language we use for this work. We also emphasize that the term, transformative justice, should be used only when separate from/not tied to law enforcement, child protective services, or any other organizations or systems tied to policing, but that are truly based on principles of liberation.

OUR BASIC APPROACH

Creative Interventions is based upon this basic approach to violence intervention and prevention:

- **Stop Violence Where It Starts.** We believe that change takes place where violence first occurs – in relationships, families, and communities. We believe that change makers, those who are the true experts, are those most impacted by violence: survivors, their friends, families, and communities – and, ultimately, the people who have caused harm.

- **Mobilize Those Closest to and Most Impacted by Violence.** We need an approach to violence prevention and intervention that builds upon mobilizing those most impacted by violence and provides multiple points at which people can collectively take action to stop violence before it occurs, or before it reaches a crisis. We need an approach that addresses and transforms the conditions and behaviors that lead to and escalate violence in the first place.

- **Build Resources for Community-Based Responses and Transformative Justice.** We believe that friends, family, and community members know most intimately the conditions that lead to violence, as well as the values and strengths which can lead to its transformation. Creative Interventions provides stories and tools to support collective, creative, and flexible solutions, which take into account the realities and resources of each situation and community.

OUR PRINCIPLES

- **Community-based:** Organized and carried out by friends, family, neighbors, coworkers, or community members rather than social services, the police, child welfare, or government institutions.

- **Facilitated or Anchored:** A person or people tied to the community where violence happened acts as a facilitator or anchor for the process.

- **Action-oriented:** Takes action to address, reduce, end, or prevent violence.

- **Collective:** A coordinated effort of a group of people. Links people and actions together to work toward the same goals with a common purpose. It sees us as a group or team rather than individuals working as lone heroes or rescuers.

- **Holistic:** Considers the good of everyone involved in the situation, including those harmed (survivors or victims), those who have caused harm, and community members affected by violence and harm.

  - **For the survivor:** Relies upon the consideration of the best ways to support survivors by sharing the responsibility of addressing violence, without blaming a survivor's choices, and by supporting a survivor to define their own needs.

  - **For the person who caused harm:** Relies upon the consideration of the best ways to support people doing harm to recognize, end, and be responsible for violence (accountability) without giving them excuses (colluding) or denying their humanity (demonizing).

- **For allies or community members:** Relies upon the consideration of the best ways to gather and mobilize the community to take accountability for their role in minimizing, denying and encouraging violence, and turn them toward supporting survivors and those who have caused harm.

- **Centers those most affected by violence** for transformative change: Recognizes that the process of changing violence, repairing from violence, and creating new ways of being free from violence takes time. Provides ways for those most affected by violence and causing violence to develop new skills and insights to put together a solution to violence, or to form a system that may reduce the chances that violence will continue.

OUR VALUES

Creative Interventions developed this version of the community-based intervention approach not only to end violence, but to lead to healthier ways of being in community with each other. We developed this list to guide us in our own work. These values underlie our vision and practice and are reflected throughout this Workbook. You can use this as a guide for your individual and collective values. See the "My Values" and "Our Values" worksheets in the "Getting Ready" section starting on page 33.

1. **Creativity.** Solutions to violence can emerge out of a creative process.

2. **Collectivity or Community Responsibility.** We believe that violence is not an individual problem and that solutions also cannot be individual. It takes all of us to end violence. The actions of a group (if done well) can be much wiser, healthier, more effective, and longer-lasting than those carried out by an individual. Collective action moves us away from relying on or acting as individual heroes and rescuers.

3. **Holism.** Solutions to violence can involve consideration for the health and well-being of everyone involved in and affected by violence – this includes the survivors or victims of violence; people doing harm; and friends, family, and community. We also want our solutions to keep communities whole. This does not necessarily mean that abusive relationships or families need to stay together, but this does mean that the people in them may be able co-exist peacefully in the same community.

4. **Safety.** We are interested in creating safety in all of its forms (physical, emotional, sexual, economic, spiritual, and so on). We honor that people, especially survivors and those most impacted by violence, define safety – rather than relying upon what the police, politicians, media, social workers, and others define as safety.

5. **Risk-Taking.** While we prioritize safety, we also believe that it sometimes takes risks to create more safety in the long-run. Safety may require action that has the potential to increase short-term risk or danger in order to reach long-term goals.

6. **Accountability.** All of us have our own role and responsibility to take in ending violence. Community-based solutions to violence require that we all step up and think about the ways we may have contributed to violence, the ways we may need to acknowledge and make amends for our contribution to violence, and the ways we can take action to make sure that violence does not continue and that healthy alternatives can take its place.

7. **Transformation.** We believe that everyone involved in violence can go through positive change. What is needed is a model for taking action that believes that healthy change is possible for all – and that can also take realistic and sometimes difficult steps to create an environment in which long-term change can be supported.

8. **Flexibility.** Situations of violence are often complicated and so are the steps toward long-term change. We try to remain flexible so that we can make changes and create new strategies when needed.

9. **Patience.** Violence is built over time and so the solution to violence takes time. We ask people to step out of expectations of quick results and take the time to create thoughtful solutions to violence, solutions that will hold in the long run.

10. **Building on What We Know (Organic).** We believe that we all as individuals, families, friendship networks, communities, and cultures have a history of creative and community-based ways to resolve violence. We want to remember, honor, and build upon the positive things we have known and done throughout history.

11. **Sustainability.** We need to support each other to create change in ways that can last over the time it takes to successfully intervene in violence. We encourage that solutions to violence are built to last over the course of the intervention, over our lifetimes, and throughout future generations.

12. **Regeneration.** We can all contribute to expanding opportunities to challenge violence and contribute to liberation. Although any of us may be thinking of our own unique situation of violence when creating a community-based response to violence, our successes lead to new changes and transformations for everyone involved. And our stories can be passed on to others so they can learn from our experiences. We ask you to consider sharing your intervention stories and lessons learned through the Creative Interventions website, the StoryTelling & Organizing Project, and through other community spaces. (See the "Additional Resources" section at the end of this book for further information.)

BASICS EVERYONE SHOULD KNOW

SOME KEY TERMS

Accountability: The ability to recognize, end, and take responsibility for violence. For all people involved, thinking about the ways they may have contributed to violence, recognizing their roles, acknowledging the ways they may need to make amends for their actions and make changes to ensure that violence does not continue and that alternatives can take its place. We see accountability as a process, one that takes time, rather than a one-time event. We see accountability as something that people often dodge and deny, especially at the beginning, and we believe that this workbook supports us in creating better opportunities and conditions for people to actually move toward meaningful accountability – even if they do not take accountability at first.

Community: We use this broadly to refer to groups of people with whom we are connected – as family, friends, neighbors, co-workers, congregations, political organizations, and so on. We do NOT mean the police (even if it's called "community policing"), the child welfare system, the government, or even organizations that might be called "community-based" – unless those organizations are directly involving survivors in collective processes. We understand that for many people, their community may be just a couple or a very few people. We also know that communities can encourage violence – or be the first to deny or minimize violence, or to blame the victim. This workbook provides guidance to identify helpful members of our communities and guidance for them to be better supporters. Note: Our notion of community is similar to pods. Learn more from the Bay Area Transformative Justice Collective's pod mapping worksheet (see the "Additional Resources" section at the end of this book).

Community accountability: A process in which a community, such as family, friends, neighbors, co-workers, or community members work together to transform situations of harm. This can also describe a process in which the community recognizes that they are impacted by violence, even if it is primarily between individuals; that they may have participated in allowing the violence to happen or even in causing the violence; and that they are responsible for resolving the violence.

Community ally or ally: Community allies or, more simply, allies are people who may not be the person directly experiencing or causing harm but who may be in their circle or community/pod. Sometimes also called "bystanders," these are all of us who might be family members, friends, co-workers, neighbors, and/or community members who know and care about the people harmed and/or the people causing harm. Often, allies are the ones who can gather to actually intervene in and prevent further harm. This workbook is aimed toward supporting community allies along with the survivor/victim and the people who have caused harm. You may also use other terms – perhaps "team" or "pod" will be more useful terms to use in your situation.

Person or people who caused harm: The primary person or people committing harm in a situation of interpersonal violence. Other people may also have caused harm, perhaps in a less direct way, by encouraging or tolerating harm or by discouraging efforts to confront harm. We aim to avoid the language of the criminal legal system and or labels. (For example, we do not say "batterer," "abuser," "perpetrator," "rapist.") Generally, we say "person who caused harm" but usually, we will use someone's name. However, we may still specifically name the harm, e.g., the word "rape." Those using this workbook can edit to use people's names, not labels. (Note: Make agreements about using names and sharing information to keep safety and confidentiality.)

Processes (also known as **community accountability** or **transformative justice processes** or **circles** – use the term that fits you): Some of us understand these types of interventions to be longer-term processes that might help us move through harm, prepare for actions, collectively build goals and strategies, support survivor(s) or victim(s), and/or support the person or people who caused harm to take accountability. In some cases, these interventions might lead to gatherings (meetings, circles, etc.) that bring together the survivor(s) and the person(s) who have caused harm. While this workbook is useful for both rapid response and processes, we think it is helpful to distinguish between the two, and for those intervening, to clarify whether they are dealing with a rapid response or a longer process.

Rapid response: Sometimes we find ourselves needing to react and respond quickly to a crisis involving harm or the threat of harm. The term rapid response distinguishes these kinds of actions from a longer, more intentional process of accountability and transformative change (see processes above).

Survivors or victims: Some people experiencing violence prefer to think of themselves as survivors and others as victims. Some use the language of "person harmed." Many people will simply want to be referred to by their name and not by either term. We will use the term "survivors and victims" throughout. Where space is limited, we use the single term "survivor." You can edit worksheets in this workbook (or that you've downloaded from our website) to use people's names, not labels. (Note: Make agreements about using names and sharing information to keep safety and confidentiality.)

SOME BASICS ABOUT INTERPERSONAL VIOLENCE

We may often hear about domestic, sexual, and other forms of interpersonal violence, but it is often misunderstood. The lack of information can lead us to blame victims, excuse people causing harm, or sometimes just turn the other way. The following provides some very basic education for everyone. We encourage you to read **Section 2 of the *CI Toolkit*** for an expanded version of the basics below.

Basic One: **Interpersonal violence usually takes place between people who know each other – sometimes making it complicated or confusing.** It can occur between people in intimate relationships, family, friends, neighbors, roommates, co-workers, members of the same organization, etc. Because these relationships may also include love, companionship, friendship, loyalty, and/or dependence or survival, the dynamics of harm may be confusing to understand and to change.

Basic Two: **Interpersonal violence can look many different ways and can take many different forms.** Examples include: physical violence or threats, verbal and emotional violence, isolation, sexual violence, economic or financial abuse, controlling property or pets, stalking, manipulating children or threatening friends and family, using homophobia or transphobia to threaten an LGBTQ+ person, threatening to call ICE against an immigrant.

Basic Three: **Interpersonal violence is often about using a pattern of power and control,** rather than anger, passion, or loss of control. We find interpersonal violence often: is one-sided, attempts to control others or get one's own way, takes advantage of vulnerability, continues in a pattern or cycle, may be calculated (even if it does not look like it), and may increase over time.

Basic Four: **Using violence as self-defense is not the same as using violence to gain or maintain power and control.** In some cases, it may be hard to tell who is acting in self-defense. This model includes some tools to help your group to unpack a complicated situation (see: Section A, "Getting Clear").

Basic Five: **Interpersonal violence is serious and common.** The direct and ripple effects of abusive and controlling behavior can be devastating. We are all impacted in some way by the pervasiveness of interpersonal violence.

CREATIVE INTERVENTIONS WORKBOOK

Basic Six:

Interpersonal violence hurts all of us – in different ways. *For survivors or victims,* it can lead to physical injury, including death; chronic health conditions; unwanted pregnancy or loss of pregnancy; loss of income or housing; emotional damage; lost sense of identity; fear of bringing danger to others; loss of love for the person who is harming us; and loss of ability to take care of others, protect children, work effectively, live a healthy spiritual life, contribute to the community, or plan for the future. *For people who have caused harm,* it can lead to: having others fear and hate us; an inability to be close to people or to be trusted; or fears that we will lose people, be abandoned, or that we are like those who were violent against us. *For people in the community,* it can lead to fear of violence; acceptance of violence as a community norm; stress and worry about people involved; fractions and divisions in communities; physical danger; or threat to income if we rely on people involved. *For everyone,* it can lead to feelings of shame and guilt; loss of self-respect; inability to trust; hopelessness; and despair.

Basic Seven:

Interpersonal violence is often hidden, denied, or ignored. Survivors may not want to talk about it or may have been threatened not to tell anyone. Community members often would rather not challenge violence, think it is okay, or perceive it as others' personal business. Society does not want to recognize it, normalizes or glorifies it, or may think it cannot be stopped.

Basic Eight:

Our personal biases and experiences can influence how we understand a situation – in good ways and bad. We are influenced by our own experiences and histories of violence, and the ways violence plays out in our communities. Your experiences may make you especially useful or knowledgeable. It can also make certain roles difficult for you to take.

Basic Nine:

We can all take steps to address, end, or prevent interpersonal violence by changing views of violence, becoming more aware of harmful reactions to violence, identifying denial in ourselves and others, challenging the tendency to minimize violence, noticing and changing "victim blaming" thoughts and attitudes in ourselves and others.

Basic Ten:

It is important to share information about interpersonal violence, as many people can benefit from being more aware. Share this workbook and other resources with survivors, people who caused harm, friends and family, and anyone who wants to get involved in working to end and prevent violence.

HOW IS A COMMUNITY-BASED RESPONSE DIFFERENT?

Usual violence intervention approach	Community-based approach
Assumes that survivors or victims want to or should separate from the people who caused harm	Explores options for survivors to stay in their relationships if desired, or supports safe co-existence in the same community.
Works only with or primarily with the survivors or victims of violence	Centers survivors, as well as friends, family members, neighbors, co-workers, or other community members (as community allies) as those best equipped to determine the best strategies for safety, accountability, and long-lasting change. Considers the person who caused harm as a potential ally in ending violence – even if not at this moment.
Tells survivors that calling the police or 911 is the safest way to end violence. Requires a report to child protective services if resource providers think that a child is being harmed – even if the provider does not believe child protective services will be helpful.	Brings intervention and prevention skills and knowledge to survivors and community allies rather than relying on authorities or "experts" to intervene.
Deals with people who caused harm primarily through the police or criminal legal system, civil legal system (e.g. restraining orders), or concepts of punishment. Discourages people to deal directly with people who caused harm in any other way.	Envisions change for and accountability of people who caused harm through making connections to what's important and meaningful to them (e.g. values, relationships, sense of identity) rather than through force, punishment, or shaming. Rejects criminal legal language such as "perpetrator" or "offender" in favor of language focused on behavior that can be changed (e.g., "person who caused harm" or "people doing harm").

SOME IMPORTANT LESSONS ABOUT INTERVENTIONS

We discovered some important lessons as we supported and witnessed different interventions to violence. While there are undoubtedly many more lessons, we wanted to share some basics. We encourage you to see the *CI Toolkit*, **Section 2**, for a more expanded version of the lessons below.

Lesson One:

Keep survivors at the center of concern. Understand that a survivor's perspective is unique; keep them in the loop of what is happening. Make sure that survivors are connected with friends, family, or community (not just therapists or counselors, though they can be included), and do not make survivors always ask for help. Make it easy, anticipate needs, offer your help and keep it up, get others to share responsibilities.

Lesson Two:

Most of us struggle with accountability. We need to create responses that take resistance and struggle into account. Anticipate a process of dodging and delaying accountability by creating systems flexible enough to allow for this process and strong enough to withstand and diminish these tactics over time. Identify the appropriate people and processes that can support people doing harm through the expected dynamics of dodging and delaying – while holding firm and challenging these tactics.

Lesson Three:

Most of us are either uncomfortable with conflict or are too comfortable with conflict. Reflect on your conflict style, be honest with yourself and others, and think about changing your relationship to conflict to contribute to a positive process.

Lesson Four:

It is important to be aware of our own agenda and biases. Community-based interventions rely upon us knowing each other and being connected to our communities. Being close to people can also bring in your own agenda and biases, which may not be helpful to the process. Reflect, be aware, and make necessary shifts so you can support the collective good.

Lesson Five:

Building teams and coordinating responses requires ample in-person time to share and build group decision-making. Today's society does not teach us about collective processes. It teaches us to do things quickly and on our own. Take the time to discuss, share opinions, uncover differences, and discover commonalities. As much as possible, do this in person (not over text). Interpersonal violence is complicated; sometimes the right answers are only discovered through the process of self-reflection and dialogue with others.

Lesson Six:

Be aware that danger can escalate when someone is about to seek safety or help. We may find that the person who caused harm may escalate threats or violence when they feel like they might lose power and control. Plan for extreme, even unimaginable situations – and work toward the safety of all involved.

Lesson Seven:

Change is difficult; transformation takes time. Everyone wants a quick fix, but we have found that change often takes time, goes through cycles, moves forward and backward, and can often lead to situations getting worse before they get better. Make room for ups and downs, create support for everyone to last through hard times, and celebrate the small successes.

Lesson Eight:

Change is difficult; little steps can be important. Community-based actions and processes can take time. Think about the small things that have helped you in times of need. Sharing concerns, caring, connection, and common feelings of powerlessness – in even small ways – can make an important and even critical difference.

Lesson Nine:

Mental health issues and/or substance abuse can make interventions difficult but not impossible. Mental health issues and substance abuse can be connected to violent behavior, and can also increase vulnerability to violence. Violence and the constant threat of violence – including interpersonal and community violence but also the trauma resulting from oppression (racism, sexism, homophobia, transphobia, ableism, anti-immigrant oppression, discrimination against people with mental health issues, etc.) – is also the cause of mental health issues and substance abuse. Raise your awareness. Approach from a position of care and support. Look for resources on disability justice, harm reduction, and healing justice.

Lesson Ten:

Interventions can bring about positive change – but can never make up for the original harm. For many of us, we may find that we have an unconscious goal to make the original situation of harm disappear. We may unknowingly believe that undoing the harm is the only thing that will make us feel satisfied. We may be disappointed when an intervention cannot do the impossible. We understand this as a natural feeling and ask for those involved to reflect, be honest with these feelings, be aware that positive changes are possible – even if we cannot undo the initial harm – and know that wanting the harm to disappear is understandable even if unattainable.

WHAT THIS IS NOT

This is NOT a recipe for violence intervention. This approach is not for everyone or for every situation. There are times when there are simply not enough resources to make this approach safe enough or likely enough to turn out a positive outcome. There are times when individuals or groups do not share enough common values to make this the right model.

This is NOT a guarantee for successful violence-intervention outcomes. There is no way to predict a positive outcome – especially for something as complex as violence. Situations change, people change, events are unpredictable. Even groups that work well together may not get the outcomes they want – especially in the long run.

This is NOT a mediation process. Mediation is a process by which two or more people or representatives meet together with a mediator to resolve a conflict. Although one person or party may feel violated by another, there is generally a sense that they have enough and equal power, and that a single process can resolve the conflict.

Mediation between the survivor or victim and person who caused harm is not recommended. The assumption that there is equal power does not match our assumptions about the types of interpersonal violence that this workbook was created to address – domestic violence and sexual assault generally take place within or create relationships of unequal power. Some mediation processes have placed "equal fault" on survivors or victims and potentially placed them in greater danger.

Mediation might be part of the overall process of intervention. For example, two allies may have a conflict about some part of the process and may have relatively equal power. A mediation process might be used to get through this conflict.

This DOES NOT require engaging the person who caused harm as part of the intervention. While we promote engagement and offer tools to support engagement, not engaging does not affect the value or success of your intervention. Some reasons to consider not engaging include:

- You might find that engagement is too risky or dangerous.
- The person who caused harm may be completely unapproachable or unwilling to engage.

- The person who caused harm may be too dangerous.

- Engaging with the person who caused harm may give them information that can make them capable of even more harm.

- You may not have the right person or people to contact and connect with the person who caused harm in a way that can bring about positive change.

- You may not know who the person who caused harm is or where they are.

This DOES NOT mean that the survivor or victim needs to have any contact with the person who caused harm, even if the community allies decided to engage the person doing harm.

The survivor or victim should never be pressured to make contact. Many sources may create pressure: guilt; duty; needs to forgive, show toughness, or show love and care; desire to be part of a team, etc. Creative Interventions believes these are never reasons enough to force contact for anyone. Making contact is a potentially risky choice and should be made carefully, with plenty of safeguards before, during, and after.

Contact between survivor and person doing harm may bring about risk or danger by:

- Re-exposing the survivor to unnecessary memories of the harm;

- Re-exposing the survivor to direct emotional, physical, sexual, financial harm, or other forms of harm by the person who caused harm (and possibly by others who might blame the survivor or want to harm them);

- Exposing the survivor to retaliation;

- Exposing the whereabouts of the survivor – if the whereabouts have been or need to be kept confidential or secret;

- Exposing the survivor to a process where their own truthfulness or integrity could be called into question – if safeguards are not made to ensure that the process is not set up to question or attack the survivor.

If the survivor decides to have contact with the person who caused harm, then the possible risks should be fully taken into account. We suggest that before considering engagement, the survivor and allies weigh risks against benefits, make safety precautions, and use this workbook and other resources to identify and address safety concerns (see Section B, "Staying Safe"). We encourage you also to see the expanded section on Safety in the *CI Toolkit*.

RAPID RESPONSE VS PROCESS

A community-based response to harm or violence can take many different forms. It may be a long-time survivor of intimate partner violence who finds the level of violence escalating, and who reaches out to friends or family members for help. It may be someone who was sexually assaulted by someone they had been dating last year, and who wants support to confront this person and make sure that they understand what they did and to never do it again. It might be someone wanting support to open up to their family members about sexual abuse committed by a family member years ago, and who also fears that this person may be harming other people in the family.

Each of these situations may require hearing the details of the story and better understanding the nature of harm and danger. People planning what to do may ask who could be helpful in figuring out how to address the harm. They may all raise concerns about safety: for some, it may be about immediate danger; for others, the immediate danger may no longer be an issue, but there may still be fears about being believed, being blamed, possible retaliation, or concerns about conflict and pain by simply raising the issue.

The community-based approach and tools in this *Creative Interventions Workbook* can address any of these concerns regardless of whether the harm was from long ago or if the harm and dangers are more immediate. The distinction between rapid response and a longer-term process may be important to make. One of the primary distinctions may be whether a response should be immediate, requiring actions to quickly gain safety, or whether the response can be somewhat slower and take more planning, perhaps leading to a process where people might meet over the course of weeks, months, or even longer in order to plan, coordinate, and support long-term change.

While something requiring a rapid response may also transition into a longer term process, there are times when a rapid response is as far as a community-based intervention, community accountability, or transformative justice response gets. The rapid response may be needed in order to achieve more immediate goals, such as creating safety. For example, supporting accountability and long-term change for the person or people who caused harm may simply not be possible. For those of us invested in the values of long-term transformation, rapid response actions that do not seem to reach the longer term goals of transformation can be disappointing – or raise questions about whether they align with the values of community accountability or transformative justice at all.

Are you looking at a rapid response? If so, make sure your steps, goals, and expected timeline are fitting what you can expect to do in the short term.

TOOLS AND WORKSHEETS

HOW TO USE THESE TOOLS

The community-based intervention is rarely a one-time event. It is a process that can take time. It may sometimes seem to move one step forward and two steps back. An intervention involves engaging people with their own unique perspectives about the situations, different goals and hopes for outcomes, and different ideas about what a process looks like. Some people may also be strongly resistant to change. An intervention can involve strong emotions (e.g., excitement, fear, shame, disappointment, frustration, relief) and can be unpredictable, as people can change their minds, attitudes, and course(s) of action or behavior.

The tools in this workbook attempt to take these factors into account. The model and tools are based on the values of creativity and flexibility, and the ability to stay on course for the long run as the intervention goes through twists and turns. The tools help gather and coordinate many different people, and an early consideration of values and goals helps the group move forward.

Three Core Areas:

Survivor/victim Support	Providing for emotional and physical health and safety and other needs and wants of a survivor of harm, which may extend to children, elders, pets, and others who rely on the survivor.
Accountability of the person who caused harm	The act of the person causing harm to recognize, end, and take responsibility for the violence and harm one has caused – regardless of whether that harm is intended – and changing attitudes and behaviors so violence will not continue.
Community accountability or social change	The work of communities to also recognize, end, and take responsibility for violence by becoming more knowledgeable, skillful, and willing to take action to intervene in violence and support social norms and conditions that prevent violence from happening in the first place.

CREATIVE INTERVENTIONS WORKBOOK 🌀

MODEL OVERVIEW & TOOLS

	TOOLS & WORKSHEETS
Getting Ready	• Checklist: Is This Right for You? • Worksheet: My Values • Worksheet: Our Values • Four Phases on the Ground • Creative Interventions Model at a Glance • Facilitator or Anchor Person • Mix & Match the Tools
Getting Clear	• Worksheet: What is going on? • Worksheet: Survivor or Person Who Caused Harm?
Staying Safe	• Types of Safety Concerns • Worksheet: My Safety • Worksheet: Risk Assessment • Worksheet: Levels of Danger • Worksheet: Safety Plan • Worksheet: Safety Follow-Up Plan • Checklist: Escape to Safety
Mapping Allies & Barriers	• Worksheet: My People • Worksheet: My People Map • Checklist: Being a Good Ally
Goal-Setting	• Matching Goals with Process • Worksheet: My Wants, My Goals • Worksheet: Making Requests • Worksheet: My Goals for Intervention/Process/Circle • Breaking Down Goals • Worksheet: Our Wants, Our Goals

TOOLS & WORKSHEETS

Supporting Survivors

- Types of Support for the Survivor or Victim
- Chart: Survivor or Victim Participation in an Intervention
- What if the Survivor Is Not Involved?

Taking Accountability

- Accountability as a Process
- Tips for Taking Accountability
- Pathway of Change or Accountability
- Worksheet: Pathway of Change or Accountability
- Worksheet: Survivor Participation in Taking Accountability
- Self-Reflection Questions for Survivors & Allies in Taking Accountability
- Worksheet: Self-Reflection Questions & Practice for Allies
- Worksheet: Self-Reflection Questions for People who Have Caused Harm
- Worksheet: My Accountability Statement

Working Together

- Tips for Working Together
- Checklist: Team Roles
- Worksheet: Agreements for Sustaining Over Time

Keeping on Track

- Worksheet: How Are We Doing? Group Guiding Questions
- Closure
- Worksheet: Our Plan for Closure

GETTING READY

It is best to think about your individual and collective values now – before you are faced with a crisis situation of harm or violence – or as you begin to figure out how you are going to deal with a situation that you are facing.

Looking at the Creative Intervention Values on page 14 or at basic transformative justice beliefs (also see Bay Area Transformative Justice Collective / BATJC, listed in "Additional Resources," for an example of their values) can get you to begin thinking about whether you hold these values, particularly when it comes to interpersonal violence and harm. If you do not – for example, if you think that it is important to call the police in the face of harms that would be considered criminal (for example, physical and sexual violence) – then you can use this workbook and other resources to think about this more deeply. You may come to realize that you do not want to participate in this type of intervention at all. It is good to be clear.

Perhaps you do believe in these values in the abstract or in some cases, but you are not sure if you do with respect to a particular situation of violence you are experiencing or that you are facing as a friend, family member, or community member. Again, it is important to use this workbook and other resources to think about your values more deeply and see if you can and should move forward to take action using this approach.

You do not all have to be on the exact same page in terms of values, but values (as well as goals) need to have some alignment. If they clash and are at great odds with each other and/or with this approach, then you may have trouble successfully addressing, reducing, ending, or preventing violence. On the other hand, even values that are initially at odds with each other can move toward alignment if you have a chance to reflect on them individually and honestly discuss them as a group.

We encourage you to start with an assessment of your values following these steps:

1. Review the Creative Interventions Values (page 14) and Transformative Justice beliefs (page 11) to understand the values underlying this approach and see how they align.

2. Look at the values on the Is This Right for You? checklist (in the "Getting Ready" section) and make sure you have common agreement.

3. Use the My Values worksheet (also in the "Getting Ready" section) to reflect on your own values (and have each person possibly working on an intervention do the same).

4. Come together with those you are working with collectively to compare and discuss your individual values – share and discuss your My Values worksheets.

5. See if you can agree on a common set of values using the Our Values worksheet.

GETTING READY

Checklist:
IS THIS RIGHT FOR YOU?

This is a basic checklist to see if your values are a good match with this approach – meaning a Creative Interventions community-based intervention approach, or what some call community accountability or transformative justice.

Use this as you are facing a particular situation of violence – you might generally agree with this approach but find that you cannot hold these values for a particular situation of violence. The important thing is to be honest.

You can also use this checklist when thinking about bringing in others to support you. Feel free to add values that will be important to you in creating a group or team to come together to address harm or violence.

Think and reflect. Can you hold these values when facing this situation of harm?

❐ Commitment to address, reduce, end, and/or prevent interpersonal violence.

❐ Value participation in a collective response including listening and learning, good communication, and clear decision-making.

❐ Lean into care, compassion, and connection rather than punishment or shaming (even if there are also feelings of anger, hatred, etc.).

❐ Will not address harm by using harm or violence.

❐ Will not rely on police or other systems (such as ICE or child welfare).

❐ Other value:

❐ Other value:

❐ Other value:

Worksheet:
MY VALUES

This worksheet can help you to reflect on and get clearer about your values. See Our Values (Creative Interventions) (page 14) or Bay Area Transformative Justice Collective (in "Additional Resources" at the end of this book) for examples.

Values Reflections and Brainstorm

The following values are important to me in my life:
(List values. Describe briefly.)

When I think about my values in how I want to deal with this situation of harm, I would add these values (or use these values instead):

GETTING READY

My Most Important Values for Addressing This Situation

Look at the values you wrote in your brainstorm – and use this sheet to prioritize your most important values as you face this situation. You can also use this section to prepare for a specific part of a process (e.g., meeting with your supporters, or going into a gathering or a circle).

Most Important Values to Me:

After making your list, you can get more specific, thinking of your most important value.

1. Highlight, circle or underline your top three most important values.

2. Reflect on each, then mark your most important value with a star.

NOTE: It is common to have strong feelings come up as you do this and other exercises. Rage, frustration, sadness, fear, disillusionment, and hopelessness are among the feelings people face. Think about what you can do to go through this in a way that is manageable and grounding. Who can you turn to for support? Is there someone who can be there with you as you go through this and other exercises?

CREATIVE INTERVENTIONS WORKBOOK

Worksheet:
OUR VALUES

This worksheet can help you as a group to reflect on and get clearer about your values. You can refer to Our Values (Creative Interventions) (page 14) or Bay Area Transformative Justice Collective (in "Additional Resources" at the end of this book) for examples.

Our Values for Addressing This Harm

The following values are important to us as a group:

Share everyone's values from their most important values for addressing this harm (see the My Values worksheet on page 35). Describe briefly to make sure people have the same understanding of what those values mean.

It can be a useful exercise for each person to pick their most important value and have them describe a situation in which this showed up as a value. NOTE: It is important to choose examples completely outside of this situation of harm – otherwise, feelings about this situation may distract from naming and sharing values – or naming of values can be used as ammunition (or perceived that way), rather than as a sincere effort to share insights and establish common ground.

GETTING READY

Our Most Important Values for Addressing This Harm

Look at the values you collected from everyone. Then use this worksheet to list and prioritize your most important values as you face this situation of violence and work toward a positive intervention, resolution, or transformation.

Our Most Important Values (write them down and make sure that everyone has the same understanding of what they mean)

After making your list, you as a group can get more specific, thinking of your most important value or values.

1. Highlight, circle, or underline your top three most important values.

2. Reflect on each, then mark your group's most important value with a star (if narrowing it seems helpful).

CREATIVE INTERVENTIONS WORKBOOK

FOUR PHASES ON THE GROUND

Interventions are generally processes made up of many steps along the way. These phases can go in cycles during the course of an intervention. You may get started, plan/prepare, take action, and follow up many times as you move along.

Getting Started

- Initiated by anyone: a survivor, family member, friends, community ally, or the person doing harm.
- Involves first steps, such as: naming the violence, mapping people and resources to help, mapping potential barriers to help, and setting initial goals.
- Thoughtful consideration of risks and how to increase safety.

Planning & Preparation

- Involves bringing people together to participate.
- Create agreed-upon values, goals, and roles for everyone.
- Create an accountability plan (if it is one of the goals).
- Thoughtful consideration of risks and how to increase safety.

Taking Action

- Deliberate and coordinated steps in violence intervention.
- Take steps to support survivors; engage with people doing harm; bring together community; improve understanding and response among friends, family, and community.
- Thoughtful consideration of risks and how to increase safety.

Following Up

- Deliberate and coordinated process following each step and phase, or at the end of an intervention.
- Can involve everyone or smaller groups.
- Make sure you are keeping on track, making plans to respond if violence happens again, and checking in to see how things are going after an intervention comes to a close.
- Should happen even if steps are never taken or things go differently than planned.
- As in all steps, thoughtful consideration of risks and how to increase safety.

On the next two pages, please see what we call the **Creative Interventions Model At a Glance**, which organizes the tools and accompanying questions by the stage. Some people have used the following two pages as a kind of guide/worksheet. Please also see Philly Stands Up's one-page version on page 9.

Tools and Worksheets

CREATIVE INTERVENTIONS MODEL AT A GLANCE

GETTING STARTED	PLANNING & PREPARATION

Getting Clear:
- What is going on?
- What kinds of violence happened or are happening?
- Who is getting harmed?
- Who is doing the harming?
- What can be done?

Getting Clear:
- What has happened since last time?
- What changed?
- What new barriers are there?
- What new opportunities are there?
- What do we need to do next?

Staying Safe:
- What are the risks now?
- What are the risks with no action?
- What are the risks if we take action?
- What do people need for safety now?
- What plans can be made for safety?
- Who can play what roles?

Staying Safe:
- What are the risks now? Any new risks?
- What are the risks with next action(s)?
- How is safety planning working?
- What are new safety needs?
- Who can play that role?

Mapping Allies & Barriers:
- Who can help? Who might get in the way?
- Who can support the survivor?
- Who can support the person doing harm?
- Who can be an ally?
- What kind of help is needed, and who can give it?

Mapping Allies & Barriers:
- Who can help? Who will contact allies?
- Who has agreed?
- Who is in the way?
- Who can be an ally (or better ally with help)?
- What kind of help is needed, and who can give it?

Goal Setting:
- What do you want? What do you not want?
- Who else can and how can others contribute to goals, if at all?
- What would you consider a success?

Goal Setting:
- Does everyone know and agree to the goals?
- Are you able to reach consensus on the goals?
- Can you state these goals as concrete steps?
- Are these goals realistic? Do they align with values?

Supporting Survivors:
- What violence did the survivor experience?
- What harms have resulted?
- What do you think will be helpful to them?
- Who can best offer this support?
- How are they getting ongoing support?

Supporting survivors:
- How does the survivor want to be involved?
- What kind of support do they need?
- Who can best offer this support?
- How are they getting ongoing support?

Taking Accountability:
- What could make the violence stop?
- What could prevent further violence?
- Who/what does the person doing harm care about?

Taking Accountability:
- What is the goal of engagement?
- What reparations are requested/offered?
- Who is offering support/connection?
- Who does what? When?
- Did you roleplay possible responses?

Working Together:
- Who needs to be here? Who is willing to be here?
- Who will contact whom?
- What do they need?
- Who should not know that you're here?

Working Together:
- Who can work together?
- Does everyone know and agree with the goals?
- What are their roles?
- How will you communicate and coordinate?
- How will you make decisions?

Keeping on Track:
- Are we ready to take the next step? How did it go?
- What did you achieve?
- Did we celebrate our achievements?

Keeping on Track:
- How did the last step(s) go?
- What did you achieve?
- Did you celebrate your achievements?
- What are the next steps? Who will do what? When? How?

CREATIVE INTERVENTIONS WORKBOOK

CREATIVE INTERVENTIONS MODEL AT A GLANCE

TAKING ACTION

Getting Clear:
- What's happened since last time? What changed?
- What new barriers are there?
- What new opportunities are there?
- What do you need to do next?

Staying Safe:
- What are the risks now? Any new risks?
- What are the risks with the next actions?
- How is the safety plan working?
- What are new safety needs? Who can play what role?

Mapping Allies & Barriers:
- Who is ready and willing to help?
- Are there roles to still be filled?
- Are there allies who can step into those roles?
- Have any allies become a barrier?
- Who can be an ally or better ally with help?
- What kind of help and who can give it?

Goal Setting:
- Are the goals still realistic?
- Does everyone know and agree with the goals?
- What goals have you reached?

Supporting Survivors:
- How is the survivor involved with the intervention?
- How is the intervention affecting them?
- What kind of support do they need and how do they want to receive it?
- Who can best offer this support?
- How are they getting ongoing support?

Taking Accountability:
- Is the team supporting a process toward accountability?
- Are there people connected to the person doing harm?
- Did the person doing harm stop their violence?
- Did they acknowledge the violence? The harms caused?
- Are they working toward repairs?
- Are they shifting attitudes and actions?

Working Together:
- Is there a working system of coordination?
- Is there a working system of communication?
- Is there a working system of decision-making?
- Is everybody working toward the same goals?
- What improvements could be made?

Keeping on Track:
- How did the last step(s) go? What did you achieve?
- Did you celebrate your achievements?
- What are your next steps?
- Who will do what? When? How?

FOLLOWING UP

Getting Clear:
- What events have happened since the beginning?
- What changes have resulted?
- Did you do what you could?

Staying Safe:
- Is the survivor safe? Do they feel safe?
- Children? Allies? Person doing harm?
- What are long-term safety plans?
- What other steps can be taken for safety?

Mapping Allies & Barriers:
- Are there new allies for the following-up phase?
- Are there new allies for ongoing monitoring? For review?
- Are there barriers to look out for in the follow-up phase?

Goal Setting:
- Have goals been met?
- What has not been met? Why not?
- Can anything be done to meet these goals?
- Can you let go of any unmet goals?

Supporting Survivors:
- Was enough support provided throughout the intervention?
- What kind of support was offered?
- What kind was most helpful?
- What kind of support is needed now?
- How are they getting ongoing support?

Taking Accountability:
- Has the person doing harm stopped violence/reduced it to a targeted level? Has future violence been prevented?
- Does the person doing harm show a strong sense of responsibility about violence?
- Has the person doing harm followed up to repair the harm?
- Is there long-term support for continued accountability?

Working Together
- Who can work together?
- Does everyone know and agree with the goals?
- What are their roles?
- How will you communicate and coordinate?
- How will you make decisions?

Keeping on Track:
- Is further intervention needed? Can the process close?
- What are the next steps? Is there a regular review?
- What happens if violence continues/starts again?
- How did you celebrate your achievements?

GETTING READY

FACILITATOR OR ANCHOR PERSON

The workbook contains many types of information and tools. We believe the model works best if someone can play the role of facilitator or anchor person (or another term that you create). The role can be taken on by more than one person or can rotate among group members as the process continues – as long as those rotating in are fully able to commit during their rotation. The facilitator does not need to be an expert or professional, but they should become familiar with the tools in this guide and in the *Creative Interventions Toolkit* and be willing to help others through them. They should have sufficient time and energy to anchor the various parts of an intervention – to make sure that things are coordinated and that there is good communication. Remember that facilitators/anchors (or anyone involved in an intervention) may need a support person or people to turn to as they move forward.

What is the role of the facilitator or anchor person?
(or use your own term)

- An anchor for people who are involved in what can be a confusing, ever-changing, and emotionally difficult situation of violence intervention.

- A guide to resources including basic information, stories, and tools, such as those included in this workbook.

- A sounding board who can ask good questions that help people figure out their own values, goals, and actions to move steps forward.

- A group coordinator who can help a group work together, share information, make decisions, and move to the next steps.

- A leader who can help move everyone forward and toward a common goal(s).

Ideally, a facilitator or anchor is familiar with and trusted by the community or people involved in the situation of violence, but not too closely or intensely involved in the situation. They should be a good communicator and good at working with groups, have values that can support the community-based intervention, and have enough time and energy for the role.

You can use the Team Roles Checklist in Section G to think through different roles for the people in your group or community, including the role of facilitator or anchor.

MIX & MATCH THE TOOLS

The following eight categories may not be a linear fit to your process.

- **A. Getting Clear.** What Is Going On?

- **B. Staying Safe.** How Do We Stay Safe?

- **C. Mapping Allies and Barriers.** Who Can Help?

- **D. Setting Goals.** What Do We Want?

- **E. Supporting Survivors or Victims.** How Can We Help?

- **F. Taking Accountability.** How Do We Change Violence?

- **G. Working Together.** How Do We Work Together as a Team?

- **H. Keeping on Track.** How Do We Move Forward?

The categories are reminders of things that your group should consider and reconsider as you move through an intervention. They contain tools that might be useful in coordinating and making sense of what can be confusing and emotional situations.

Interventions are rarely a straight course from beginning to end. You may return to the various categories of tools again and again.

Individual & Group Use of Tools

Some of these tools may work better for individuals or groups. Individuals can think about these questions beforehand, then bring reflections to the group. These questions can be useful guides for group discussions and agreements that might involve new insights for all, but may also lead to times where groups may recognize disagreement or where they cannot compromise.

A. GETTING CLEAR

Getting clear means taking the time to look around and think about what is happening. Having a clear understanding of the situation is helpful when you are first deciding to take action. This is especially important when you are in a crisis and are confused. As things change, it may be necessary to continue to assess the situation, taking snapshots along the way and noting changes as they unfold.

The big picture

Getting clear involves thinking about what you already know about the situation and learning from what others have seen or experienced in the situation. Sharing information can create a fuller picture of what is going on. Different people may have seen one piece of the situation, and may describe and understand a situation in an entirely different way. Together, you can put the pieces together and understand that you are seeing different angles of one larger reality.

The important points

Interpersonal violence can be confusing. It can be especially complicated when it involves close and sometimes long-term relationships or involves many people or dynamics of violence that unfold in multiple ways. Figuring out what is going on can be difficult. It can require us to sort through details. It may be important to lay out all the pieces first, before figuring out what the most critical points are and the patterns that are most important to try to change.

Sharing information without constant rehashing

Taking collective action toward change often involves having other people's input on the process and may involve sharing some details about the violent situation. Out of concern for privacy, confidentiality, or safety issues, not everyone needs to know every detail of the situation. However, many will want some basic information in order to decide if and how they want to get involved. Good information will help everyone make better decisions about what actions to take.

Finding a good way to write down, record, or otherwise remember those details without making someone repeat the story over and over is useful. It prevents those telling the story, especially the survivor or victim, from having to re-live the details. It also keeps track of important details that can be lost as people get tired or when it's assumed everyone already knows the details.

Worksheet:
WHAT IS GOING ON?

This worksheet can help you identify what are the key issues of violence, abuse, or harm that you or someone you are close to is facing.

How would you describe the harm that is happening or happened?
Be specific: type of harm, length of time, frequency, when it started/stopped.

Who is or was getting harmed and in which ways?
There may have been multiple people directly harmed or indirectly harmed.

GETTING CLEAR

Who is or was doing the harm and in which ways?

There may have been multiple people who directly caused harm – or who caused harm by denying, minimizing, or colluding with the harm.

How long has the harm been going on? Does it happen in cycles?

Has it been getting worse? More frequent and/or more serious?

Who knows about the situation?

Are there certain people or circumstances that make it get worse or better?

GETTING CLEAR

Have people tried to stop this harm before? Who? What did they do? What happened? What was effective?

What are some key things that you still need to find out? What are some possible steps for finding out?

GETTING CLEAR

Are there other important things to know or keep track of?

Worksheet:
SURVIVOR OR PERSON WHO CAUSED HARM?

(For When It Is Hard to Tell)

GETTING CLEAR

You may encounter situations where it can be difficult to tell who is committing violence against whom, or who is the survivor and who is the primary person doing harm. There may be cases in which violence seems to be mutual at first. However, it is more common that one person is holding power and control over another person in a pattern. Use this worksheet to try to unpack a complicated situation.

Who is more afraid?	
Who starts the violence?	
Who ends up getting harmed? (In the short-term? In the long-term?)	
Who is changing and adapting to meet another's needs or moods?	
Who is more vulnerable?	
Who is using violence for power and control? Who is using violence to try to maintain safety and integrity in an already violent situation (self-defense)?	
Whose world is getting smaller?	
Who always has to win?	

USE WITH CAUTION: This is not a test with absolute right or wrong answers. Going over these questions can support survivors to clarify the dynamics of an often complicated and confusing situation. It can help supporters/allies to better understand dynamics and prepare for support, safety planning, and accountability.

B. STAYING SAFE

You or someone you know may already be in a dangerous or harmful situation. You may need to think about very basic safety needs, such as telling trusted people about the situation of violence and taking care of medical or mental health needs. For some, escaping from the situation may be a priority.

Evaluate potential risks of harm in taking action, and not taking action.

Staying safe is a centerpiece for most violence interventions. The risk of danger to or retaliation against yourself or others is important to consider at every step. In some situations, taking action can endanger the person causing harm (self-harm or by others). These tools ask you to consider how taking action, as well as not taking action, can result in harm. It also helps you evaluate how an action could inadvertently bring harm to others.

Work with others.

Because interventions may be taken in risky or dangerous conditions, any move to take the next step should involve at least one other trusted person – and hopefully more – to help with planning, support, and follow up.

Distinguish threats to safety from feelings of discomfort, vulnerability, or shame.

Moving outside our comfort zone may make us feel insecure – but this is not necessarily a threat to safety. Feelings of discomfort because of vulnerable disclosures, uncertainty, embarrassment, or shame may be difficult but important aspects of creating safety in the long term.

KEY QUESTIONS
1. What are risks and dangers right now?
2. Who is at risk?
3. What is the level of risk or danger?
4. What are the risks & dangers of taking action?
5. What are the risks and dangers of taking no action?
6. Who needs safety & protections?
7. What plans can we make to provide safety & protection?

STAYING SAFE

Types of Safety Concerns

Safety can mean many things. This list can help you sort out the types of safety concerns you had in the past, have now, or might face moving forward.

- **Physical Safety:** physical or threatened harm to the body or to one's life, threats of harm to self or others, removal of care or support for disabled people, etc.

- **Emotional Safety:** insults, manipulation, threats, isolation, etc. – or emotional stress such as anxiety, depression, loneliness, etc.

- **Financial Safety:** loss of money, property, housing, income, employment, etc.

- **Sexual Safety:** sexual threats, aggression, coercion, or violation, etc. – or triggers and trauma from past sexual harms.

- **Spiritual Safety:** keeping you from your spiritual/faith/religious values, faith practice or faith community, coercive religious practices, etc.

- **Safety from Other Threats:** threats of using ICE/immigration control, loss of children through custody, etc., turning people against you, outing of sexual orientation or gender identity, disclosing information that could harm you, etc.

- **Safety of Loved Ones:** harm to children, family members, friends, pets, etc.

- **Other:** types of safety issues that are not listed above.

Concerns that can come up in preparation for a gathering/circle:

This is a list of normal things that people often fear:
- Fear that you will not be believed.
- Fear that you will not believe yourself.
- Fear that you will lose people you care about and love.
- Fear that you will lose resources essential to your survival.
- Fear that people will challenge you.
- Fear that people will blame you.
- Fear that people will look down on you.
- Fear that people will not come to the gathering or circle for you.
- Fear that people will bring up things that you may have done.
- Fear that loved ones will be hurt by what they hear.

CREATIVE INTERVENTIONS WORKBOOK

Worksheet:
MY SAFETY

This worksheet is to help you think about safety concerns and needs. It can also help with a safety plan. This worksheet is best done with someone you trust.

Seeking support: Thinking about safety can feel threatening and scary. Part of your safety plan can include how to let others know about your safety concerns and when to ask for support. It can also help you think through how and when you might take action to move toward a gathering or a circle and whom to include.

Grounding in our wisdom: We have all faced harms, and we all have strategies to keep safe. What are some of the ways that you have kept safe in the past or right now? This can include things that you might not want to do now, but that may have helped you before. What does this tell you about how you want to address safety in the future?

In the past, I have used these ways and these people to feel safe or safer:

Right now, these are things that I am doing that help me with safety (you can include the people you turn to):

STAYING SAFE

Moving forward, these are things I can do to address my safety, including new things to try (you can add people and actions):

CREATIVE INTERVENTIONS WORKBOOK

Worksheet:
RISK ASSESSMENT CHART

A risk assessment takes into account what has been done in the past, what is happening now, and what could happen in the future. Risk assessment also should take account of changing conditions – people coming or leaving, housing changes, job changes, school, etc. Risk assessment should also include access to and use of weapons, threats of calling systems (e.g., ICE, child protective services, etc.), and access to digital threats such as online surveillance and doxxing (publishing private information on the internet to set up others to target and escalate attacks).

Type of harm, or risk of harm (See: Types of Safety Concerns at the beginning of this section)	Cause (person or situation)	Target of risk/harm	Who is looking out for safety?

STAYING SAFE

Worksheet:
LEVELS OF DANGER

Use this worksheet to list your safety concerns and identify the level of current concern or danger. Write down as much detail as possible, as you may come back to this worksheet at a later date.

Safety concerns	Level*	Is this concern in the past, present, or future?

* 5 = very low, 4 = low, 3 = medium, 2 = high, 1 = urgent/emergency
(or use other scale that makes sense to you)

STAYING SAFE

Worksheet:
SAFETY PLAN

Return to the safety skills, wisdom and people you listed in the My Safety Worksheet above. See the My People worksheet (Section C) to consider who else can help you think about safety, come up with a safety plan, and support you with that plan.

Name the safety concern (may be from the Risk Assessment above):

What can be done to increase safety or reduce danger or harm?

STAYING SAFE

What steps can be taken?

Who can support me to:

Talk about the plan	
Take steps to make the plan	
Lend support if the threat actually comes up	

What are your next steps?

It may be helpful to include the timing and who can support you to take that step.

Step	Timing Period	Support or Action

STAYING SAFE

Do we have all the bases covered? Do we need to bring more people in?

Is there an emergency back-up plan?

What is it? Who can help support the plan? What roles can they take?	
How will we know if we should go into emergency mode?	
Is there a signal or code to let people know I need help? What is it/are they? What are the expected steps if the signal or code is given?	

CREATIVE INTERVENTIONS WORKBOOK

Worksheet:
SAFETY FOLLOW-UP PLAN

Use this worksheet to follow up on the safety plan.

How did it go? What did we learn as a team?

How does this affect our safety plan? How does it affect our intervention plans?

Are there any changes to be made? Explain.

Who needs to communicate what to whom?

STAYING SAFE

Who can know?

Who should NOT know?

STAYING SAFE

What are the next steps?

Checklist:
ESCAPE TO SAFETY

Use this worksheet if you are in a situation that may require escape. If you have children or dependents, consider how to take them with you. It can be difficult to regain custody if your children are left with your partner. This was adapted from the National Coalition Against Domestic Violence's personalized safety plan (see https://ncadv.org/personalized-safety-plan).

Remember, you have the right to live without fear and violence.

☐   Think of a safe place to go if conflict or threats start – avoid rooms with only one entry/exit (e.g. bathrooms) or rooms with weapons (kitchen, garage).

☐   Think about and make a list of safe people to contact – let them know your situation and their role.

☐   Keep cash/charge card with you at all times (consider getting untraceable prepaid charge cards as an emergency).

☐   Memorize all important phone numbers (and keep them written down in safe places and with safe people).

☐   Establish a "code word" or "signal" so that family, friends, teachers, or co-workers know when to offer or call for help.

☐   Have a plan for how to pick up children and pets safely if they are not with you when you escape (let school, sitters, etc. know immediately who is safe and who is not for pick up – let them know safe and unsafe people in advance, if possible).

☐

☐

☐

STAYING SAFE

C. MAPPING ALLIES & BARRIERS

This model is based on the idea that working collectively gives us more support, power, resources, and good ideas than working alone. It is also based on the idea that communities have a responsibility to come together to end violence and that we all benefit by creating a safer and healthier community. Mapping allies and barriers involves taking a look at who we have around us as helpers and community resources (allies) and who might get in the way of an intervention (barriers).

Mapping allies involves looking at people and organizations around you and asking: Who may play a role? They may be people close to you, or they may be people we do not know well but who can play an important role in dealing with a situation of harm. They may stick around for the long haul or play a useful role here and there. Allies can play all kinds of roles in interventions to violence. They can provide support for the survivor or victim, for the person doing harm, or for other allies playing more involved or higher risk roles. They can also provide logistical or interpersonal support to the intervention.

Getting allies for the person who caused harm is an important part of the process. Allies are **not** people who will excuse violence, feel sorry for the person doing harm, or see "their side" of the situation. They are also not there to humiliate or punish the person doing harm or ensure justice is done. They are there to support the person in recognizing, ending, and taking accountability for their violence.

Use the My People Worksheet on the next page to start mapping allies.

Another excellent resource for ally or people mapping is Bay Area Transformative Justice Collective (BATJC) and their pod-mapping worksheet (see "Additional Resources").

For survivors: Who do you go to for support? Who can listen and help you recenter yourself when you start having difficult feelings or engaging in behaviors that do not feel aligned with your values?

For people who caused harm: Who can support you to take responsibility for harm?

For community allies: Who do you want to build a team with? How can others contribute to a team culture and experience that will help you stay involved? How can you avoid people who do not have the skills to work together collectively?

Worksheet:
MY PEOPLE

Start with a list of anybody that you think of. You can select from this list later.

The people I turn to in my life...	Their strengths	Their limitations

After brainstorming, mark next to each name:

S for supporter: Person can offer kindness and care.
A for accountabllity: Person can keep you honest with yourself and others.
N for not now: Person you do not want in the circle with you right now.

MAPPING ALLIES & BARRIERS

On this page, start to prioritize the people that you want to participate as your support, in your intervention, process, or circle.

Names	Potential role	Likelihood to participate*

*Write in the likelihood that they will participate, as well as any potential barriers (live far away, might not have time, need more info).

MAPPING ALLIES & BARRIERS

CREATIVE INTERVENTIONS WORKBOOK

Worksheet:
MY PEOPLE MAP

This is a circular visual to map your people as another option.

1. **Start with people who you are surest about** (write their names),

2. **Put in people who you know but may not be your closest people**, but who you can imagine that you could turn to with some preparation or support.

3. **Put in people or perhaps organizations that you might reach out to as support**, but may be supporters who require some more outreach or exploration, or perhaps live further away.

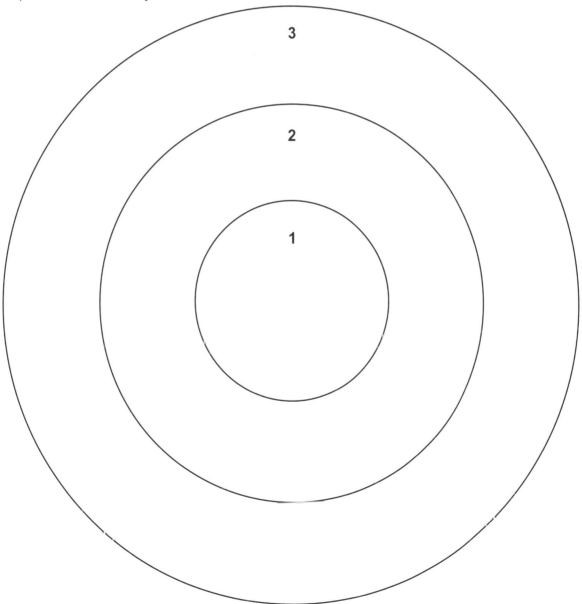

MAPPING ALLIES & BARRIERS

Checklist:
BEING A GOOD ALLY

Fill out the checklist below to see if the person you want to include will be a good ally – or to look at yourself if you are being asked to be involved.

- ❑ Is a good listener.

- ❑ Has a good understanding of dynamics of violence, or is willing to learn.

- ❑ Will not blame the survivor or victim, or will be open to understanding that blaming is not helpful.

- ❑ Can think about the person doing harm with compassion (even if they are outraged, angered, disgusted, etc.).

- ❑ Does not always have to be right – can be part of group decision-making.

- ❑ Does not always have to be the center of attention – can be a good team player.

- ❑ Is not a gossip, or at least will not gossip about this situation.

- ❑ Is a good communicator or is willing to learn how to be better.

- ❑ Is good at follow-through, or would be for this situation.

- ❑ Has some time to be available for conversations, meetings, etc.

- ❑ Other characteristics:

- ❑ Other characteristics:

MAPPING ALLIES & BARRIERS

D. GOAL SETTING

Goal setting includes the steps that individuals and groups take to move toward a single outcome or set of goals. It sets a clear direction for where you are headed, gives a guide to lead the way during times of confusion, and lets people who are involved know what they are working toward and what is expected of them.

While everyone may agree that they want violence to end, agreement may stop there, leading to points of conflict or break down. The tools in this section were created to help you think about your individual goals, consider the different ideas and goals of your group, and move toward group agreements. The tools can also help you turn vague goals into concrete ones, so that you can have a better idea of when goals are actually met. More tools for teamwork can be found in Section G, "Working Together."

Goals may be organized under one or more of the following areas.

Survivor or victim support: Focuses on the health, safety, and other needs of someone who has been harmed, and may also extend to children, family members, pets, and others who rely on the survivor or victim.

Accountability of the person doing harm: Focuses on support for the person who caused harm to recognize, end, and take responsibility for the harm one has caused, and change behaviors so the violence will not continue.

Community accountability or social change: Focuses on working with communities to recognize the ways in which they are responsible and to make changes so that harm will not continue.

GOAL SETTING IN 6 BASIC STEPS

1. Name concrete goals that individuals want and don't want.
2. Name bottom lines as the limits that individuals might have or things that they will not agree to.
3. Create group consensus or agreement on goals and bottoms lines.
4. Separate short-term and long-term goals.
5. Prioritize the most important goals; name one or two to focus on immediately.
6. Turn goals into action plans that can be revised over time.

GOAL-SETTING

Matching Goals with Process

Goal setting is closely linked to the process you plan to use – the process you plan to use is closely linked to your goals.

We understand that some people will come to use the Workbook or Toolkit without having a clear idea about what kind of process might come about. The process might emerge as you think about the situation, the people you can bring together, and the kinds of processes that you're more familiar with or that are a good fit with your culture. If this is a rapid response to get more immediate safety, then your entire "process" may simply be preparing for and taking action to gain safety. You might find that your goals are very much centered around safety and immediate support.

We also understand that some people will already have an idea of a kind of process because that's what you've heard about or used before – perhaps it's something that you've already used in other situations.

Or you may have the right conditions that can move you toward a more intentional Process – with a capital P. Some processes that people might move toward are:

- Survivor meeting together with support people to move through sections of this Workbook or Toolkit – e.g., values, naming the harms, safety, goal setting – in a way that supports the survivor but perhaps does little or nothing with the person who caused harm.

- Allies planning and moving toward engagement with the person who caused harm to make requests for safety and accountability – but that might not continue in an ongoing supportive relationship with that person.

  - This may be done in person or through other means.

- Allies holding more long-term support with the person who caused harm to engage in a process that accompanies and supports them through a journey that might lead to more substantial and long-term change. (See "Pathways of Change or Accountability" in Section F.)

- Perhaps you understand these preparations and gatherings in the form of "circles." This might mean support teams for the survivor and support teams for the person who caused harm moving separately but in ways that align with similar goals. In some cases, there may be a desire for a gathering in which all parties get together in a circle – such circles often take long-term preparation in order to get everyone ready to have the best chance of gaining a good outcome.

As you consider your goals, this might help you better determine what kind of process is desired – or what is possible.

At times, you as a group or community may simply not have all of the conditions and resources to carry out a fully engaged, long-term process.

Some things to consider in deciding upon a good process and thinking about appropriate goals include:

- Does the survivor feel it's important for them to meet with the person who caused harm (given adequate preparation and safety)? (Note: Any of these processes can happen without the survivor being present, if you are working as a coordinated team.)

- Is it important and is it possible for others to meet with the person who caused harm (with the consent of the survivor but not necessarily with their presence)?

- Is the person who caused harm willing to be engaged – even if they do not fully take accountability for the harm, at least at the beginning? (Note: It is rare to get someone to take accountability right away.)

- Do you have someone (preferably more than one person) on your team or in your group that is a good person to engage with or support the person who caused harm? If so, for how long and for what purpose? Do these people have the support they need to continue in this role?

- Are you willing and wanting to go through these steps and stages of a process even if the outcomes do not turn out to be ideal – for example, if people blame the survivor, if they lie, if they get angry, if they blame the process?

- Are you willing to face the consequences and possible risks to safety that could arise if the process goes wrong? Have you fully considered what those risks are?

- Do you have the right people, aligned values, enough time, and right conditions to get these needs or goals met? If not, what else can be done to reduce harm?

The *Creative Interventions Workbook* can help but does not fully get into the details for these more formal processes or circles. See "Additional Resources" at the end of this book for more information and supportive resources.

Worksheet:
MY WANTS, MY GOALS

Use this worksheet to brainstorm your hopes and goals. Use the "My Values" worksheet on page 35 to help you clarify your values before starting on this section.

Think about what you want or what your goals are in general. What comes up?

CREATIVE INTERVENTIONS WORKBOOK

What are your hopes or goals for this intervention, process, or circle specifically?

What are things you do NOT want?

These might be things you don't want in your life, things you do not want to happen, or things you don't want in the intervention, process, or circle.

GOAL-SETTING

Worksheet:
MAKING REQUESTS

Use this worksheet to brainstorm requests you have from a specific person or people. Add as many names as you want or need.

Name(s):

Name(s):

Name(s):

Worksheet:
MY GOALS FOR THE INTERVENTION/ PROCESS/CIRCLE

Use this worksheet to get clear about your wants and goals if you will be holding an intervention, a process, or a circle (choose any word that best fits your situation).

List your wants or goals for the intervention/process/circle. What would you consider success?

This can be "wants" for yourself or for others. Try to be clear and honest with yourself. Be specific about what and for whom.

Breaking Down Goals

Go back to your goals to see if the following are helpful in clarifying your wants and goals more. You can also come up with your own categories.

Priority or Importance

1. High priority: Wants/goals that are absolutely necessary or extremely important.
2. Medium priority: Wants/goals that are important, but I can live without.
3. Low priority: Wants/goals that I would like, but are a lower priority.

Realistic

1. Yes: Wants/goals that are reachable or realistic – even if not guaranteed.
2. Maybe: Wants/goals that might be reachable or realistic – I'm less sure.
3. No: Wants/goals that have no chance of being reachable or realistic. You might consider crossing these off the list. (Note: These may be difficult to get rid of – take time to take care of your emotions and grieve if needed; consider if and how these wants/goals could be met in another way.)

Timeline

1. Short-term: Wants/goals that could be achieved during the preparation stage or during an intervention/process/circle (or within 6 months).
2. Long-term: Wants/goals could be achieved after 6 months or that are ongoing wants/goals helped by an intervention/process/circle.

Values Alignment

1. *Aligned:* Wants/goals that meet my values. If you made a list of values using the "My Values" worksheet on page 35, start there. Otherwise, think about what your values are when you are at your best.
2. *Not Aligned:* Wants/goals that do not reflect my values. For example, you may have chosen this intervention or process or circle because you see this as an alternative to punishment, revenge, violence, arrest, imprisonment, banishment, etc. – but you may find that some of your wants/goals actually reflect punishment or shaming attitudes or actions. If your wants/goals are not aligned with your own values, consider taking them off the list.

CREATIVE INTERVENTIONS WORKBOOK

GOAL-SETTING

Worksheet:
OUR WANTS, OUR GOALS

This is a worksheet for your group to come up with wants or goals for the intervention/process/circle.

Each person can start with their "My Wants, My Goals" worksheet in Section D to think about individuals' wants and goals, then use this worksheet to create a common list of wants or goals for the circle or afterward that you can agree upon as a group.

What we hope to achieve by having the intervention/process/circle includes:

If it's useful, your group can organize your wants and goals.

- List your wants/goals in order of priority (or number them afterwards). Put a star next to those that are the highest priority.

- Put an S next to shorter-term goals that you hope to achieve right away, put an L next to longer-term goals that might be farther in the future.

- Check to see if these goals align with your values.

What we do NOT want to happen during or after the intervention/process/circle.

Look at each separately and ask yourself these questions: Do you still want to hold the intervention/process/circle even if there may be a risk of this happening? Is there preparation you need beforehand to deal with the possibility of this happening (for example, emotional preparation or actions to be taken).

CREATIVE INTERVENTIONS WORKBOOK

E. SUPPORTING SURVIVORS

Supporting survivors or victims can be the first step in addressing the harms that inter-personal violence brings. Support might focus on providing for the health, safety, or other needs and wants of the person who has directly experienced harm. It might also include providing for children, family members, and others who rely on the survivor or victim, or whose own health and safety may be affected.

Supporting survivors or victims can require patience, forgiveness, and a non-judgmental response. Survivors or victims may not always be clear or straight-forward in stating their feelings or needs. Fear of judgment from others, fear of retal-iation, self-blame, and shame, among other factors, can make it difficult to talk about violence and to ask for support. Some may have already reached out for support and received a negative response, or no response at all.

It is important to follow through. It can be easy to promise many things when a survivor or victim tells us their story. It is important to think about what you can do and evaluate your time, energy, resources, and your own safety. If you did promise some-thing that you cannot deliver, take accountability for your inability to follow through. See if you can find other ways to offer support.

Work with others so that together you can offer support that none of you could do alone. Make sure that survivor support is a central part of the intervention plan. At least one person should have the primary role of staying connected and checking in with survivor wants or needs. The group's plan should include space for a survivor to voice fears or concerns. You may not always agree with their values, opinions, or goals. It is useful to hold back when you experience feelings of judgment , blame, or frustration and examine where the feelings are coming from. Once you self-check and self-reflect, it may be important to share concerns to foster honest discussion and alignment. Use the "Our Values" and "Our Wants, Our Goals" worksheets (pages 37 and 79, respectively) to discuss and reach group agreement.

KEY QUESTIONS
1. What violence or abuse did the survivor or victim experience?
2. What harms have resulted?
3. What do they think will be helpful to them?
4. Who can best offer this support?
5. How are they getting ongoing support?

Types of Support for the Survivor or Victim

Use this tool to consider possible types of support that survivors or victims say have been or would be helpful to them. You can check off the boxes that are ways you might be able to support, or if you're the survivor, check off boxes that would be helpful for you.

❒ Let them know you care and that they are not alone.

❒ Listen to their story.

❒ Ask them what they need (so they do not have the burden of always asking for their needs to be met).

❒ Help them get what they need (without them asking each time).

❒ Let them know that interpersonal violence happens to many people.

❒ Praise them for taking action to address their situation, including talking to you.

❒ Offer a sounding board to listen or offer feedback (not necessarily advice).

❒ Offer patience for ambiguity, confusion, a changed mind.

❒ Be someone to lean on or a hand to hold through fear, confusion, shame.

❒ Support them in safety planning (see Section B).

❒ Help them access medical care, mental health care, and/or counseling.

❒ Offer religious or spiritual support.

❒ Support with children or other dependents (childcare, pick-ups, activities, emotional support for children).

❒ Take care of pets, plants, or other beings that the survivor usually cares for.

❒ Help educating and informing others to be good allies – trusted friends, family members, neighbors, co-workers, community members.

❒ Help protect from people who may bring risk or harm, including those who mean to be helpful but who are not.

❒ Help to find and make connections to resources.

❒ Help with housing or safe shelter.

❒ Help with moving, storing things, packing/unpacking.

❒ Accompany them to appointments or meetings.

❒ Offer rides/transportation.

❒ Offer access to phone or internet or other forms of communication.

❒ Help with essentials (money, food, clothing).

❒ Help figure out how they want to talk about the situation.

❒ Help figure out what they specifically need and want to prioritize.

❒ Educate yourself on medical and access needs and offer resources.

❒ Help with translation, interpretation, or explaining factors such as culture or immigration.

Survivor or Victim Participation in an Intervention

Finding where you are on this chart can help clarify the level of survivor participation – including leading, coordination, decision-making, and communication.

Survivor Leadership Level (below)	Survivor Led	Survivor Centered	Survivor Coordination & Decision-Making	Communication with Survivor
Highest level of priority	Survivor is leading and directing	Survivor goals = intervention goals	Survivor makes key decisions and coordinates allies	Survivor is making all decisions and knows all information – decides what to communicate
Priority, but consideration of others is important	Survivor is leading, but others may act in important roles (e.g., facilitator)	Survivor goals are the priority, but there is group input and agreement	Survivor is involved in all decision-making, with a process for input from others	Survivor knows all information but there is active involvement of a group with significant information
Important, but consideration weighed with others	Survivor may have started the process, but a group has agreed to shared leadership	Survivor goals are central but with consideration of allies/ community goals – use consensus	A group is coordinating decision-making and includes the survivor as key contributor	There is a group process for sharing information and communication with everyone including the survivor

SUPPORTING SURVIVORS

Survivor Leadership Level (below)	Survivor Led	Survivor Centered	Survivor Coordination & Decision-Making	Communication with Survivor
Important, but role is mostly to give feedback	Survivor has some distance – agrees to a process to give feedback	Survivor has participated and agrees with goals, but may not be involved in changes	Survivor has some distance and has agreed to a process for giving feedback	Survivor has some distance but there is an agreed process and timing for giving information
Survivor agrees but is not involved*	Survivor agrees generally but will not be involved	Survivor has participated and agrees with goals, but may not be involved if goals change	Survivor is not involved in coordination and decision-making	Survivor may or may not be given information at agreed-upon timing or at end
Survivor disagrees and is not involved*	Survivor disagrees with the intervention and is not involved	Survivor disagrees but group considers known or likely survivor goals including safety	Survivor is not involved in coordination or decision-making	Survivor disagrees and may or may not be given information to let them know what is happening
Survivor is not at all involved*	For some reason, survivor is completely unavailable	Group considers known or likely survivor goals including safety	Survivor is not involved in coordination or decision-making	Survivor if reachable may or may not be given information to let them know what is happening

*See "What If the Survivor Is Not Involved?" on page 85.

What If the Survivor Is Not Involved?

The last three rows of the grid show situations in which the survivor or victim is not involved in the intervention process. Creative Interventions has found that survivor participation is best. However, we have led situations and know of others where survivor involvement or even agreement was not present.

For example, an organization or community group may have a policy where they will take action if they learn about harm or abuse caused by someone in that organization. In some cases, the organization may have a strict "survivor-led" policy in which they will always follow the lead of the survivor – including doing nothing, if that is what the survivor desires. Or the policy may be to take action whenever they learn about certain types or levels of violence or abuse. They may let the survivor know about their policy and their responsibility to address the violence, preferably with the participation of the survivor. (We urge organizations to create policies in advance that are shared, supported, and given ample attention and resources throughout the organization.)

If the survivor is not participating or disagrees, then a community-based intervention still has the responsibility to support the survivor as best as it can. This can include:

- Continuing to meet with the survivor to see if differences can be addressed.

- Leaving an open door for the survivor to participate or check in.

- Finding a way to include their known or likely goals into the intervention goals.

- Offering support through the many options in "Supporting Survivors" (Section E).

- Offering occasional updates such as: a) requests made of the person who caused harm, b) follow up on what the person who caused harm has committed to and completed; c) results of the intervention at agreed upon time intervals and agreed upon ways, e.g., email, phone, in-person meetings, etc.

F. TAKING ACCOUNTABILITY

Accountability is the ability to recognize, end, and take responsibility for violence. We usually think of the person who caused harm as the one to be accountable for violence. Community accountability also means that communities can be accountable for sometimes ignoring, minimizing, or even encouraging violence. Communities must also recognize, end, and take responsibility for violence by becoming more knowledgeable, skillful, and willing to take action to intervene in violence, as well as support norms and conditions that prevent violence from happening in the first place. This section focuses primarily on accountability of the person who caused harm; however, the information and tools can also apply to communities that have allowed harm to happen.

There is no blueprint for accountability

Accountability means many things. It involves listening, learning, taking responsibility, and changing. It involves conscientiously creating opportunities in our families and communities for direct communication, understanding and repairing of harm, readjustment of power, and rebuilding relationships and communities toward safety, respect, and happiness. People, situations, and types of violence are different and require different responses. Some interventions work best when they are short, to the point, and allowed to show their impact over time. Other interventions do well with lots of time and intense involvement.

Accountability may not be the primary goal for every situation

Sometimes a community does not have the resources, time, or opportunity to engage a person doing harm to take accountability. Sometimes people who caused harm are not ready or willing to make any efforts to change their views or violence. Sometimes the violence committed is so morally heinous to us or it is so long-standing that we feel hatred, anger, and disgust and cannot find anyone who might engage the person doing harm without a sense of aggression or vengeance. Sometimes people doing harm show that any requests for accountability result only in escalating harmful behaviors.

You can start accountability now – any step can be useful

Even when resulting positive changes might not be immediate, visible, enough, or lasting, efforts to intervene in violence are a big deal. They rise above silence, passivity, and inaction and help make peace and wellness in our communities something we work for, not wait for.

86   **CREATIVE INTERVENTIONS WORKBOOK**

Accountability as a Process

Accountability can happen over a continuum of time.

In the short term, we might:

- Stop using violence.

- Listen to understand how our actions have impacted those around us.

- Take action to repair harm that our actions have caused others.

- Try out new ways of thinking and behaving.

- Get support and encouragement for our efforts and successes.

As a longer-term or life-long process, we might:

- Grow our confidence to face our imperfections.

- Turn away from patterns that harm others (and, ultimately, ourselves).

- Grow our ability to feel our emotions without acting them out.

- Practice and promote behaviors that honor ourselves and others.

- Humbly support others around us to do the same.

- Learn from and move beyond mistakes and setbacks.

- Practice self-awareness and self-reflection.

- Build mutually supportive and enjoyable relationships.

Accountability can happen along a continuum of depths.

Any of the following can be thought of as elements of accountability:

- Being confronted, even just once, about the violence that was done.

- Understanding that violence has negative consequences.

- Stopping or reducing violence, even if it is a result of social pressure or the threat of losing relationships, and not because of deep change.

- Listening to the person who was harmed talk about their experience of violence without being defensive, interrupting, or reacting to the story.

- Acknowledging that the use of violence was ultimately a choice, not something caused by someone else.

- Expressing sincere apology, taking responsibility, and showing care.

- Giving financial reparation or other kinds of repairs such as service.

- Agreeing to take every step to ensure that harms will not be committed again.

- Agreeing that any future acts of harm will result in negative consequences.

- Telling others about one's use of violence in order to stop hiding interpersonal violence and to ask for support in changing behaviors.

- Committing to the goal of addressing the root causes of violence, learning new skills, and deeply transforming violent behaviors.

- Showing actual changes in thinking and actions in both good and stressful times.

- Supporting others who have used violence to take steps toward accountability.

TAKING ACCOUNTABILITY

Tips for Taking Accountability

Accountability is a challenging aspect of community-based interventions to violence, community accountability, or transformative justice. Each tool in our *Creative Interventions Toolkit* has a Tips section, and we are highlighting accountability tips in our workbook, because this process is consistently challenging.

Please see the *Creative Interventions Toolkit*, Section 4F for twenty tips! We are including some of them here in shorter form for your information.

1. **Accountability is a process; it may take many types of strategies along the way.** These might include: a) communicating and showing connection and care; b) gathering community to widen connection and increase leverage; c) at times, some measure of pressure or force might be necessary to prevent further violence. We do not mean the use of physical violence. However, asking people to leave certain spaces or positions in order to achieve short-term safety is at times necessary.

2. **Make sure people keep connected to the person who caused harm.** Taking accountability is not usually an isolated act. Community contact and, at the very least, ongoing communication can support someone toward long-term change. Not connecting can raise anxiety and contribute to the dynamics that feed into abuse and violence. Connection should not be the role of the survivor of harm. This is a collective approach in which others might play the best role.

3. **Keep an eye on safety.** See "Staying Safe" (Section B).

4. **Remember that communities are also responsible for violence.** The process of a community taking accountability can serve as an important model of accountability for those who caused harm. It can also be important to a survivor who may have been directly or indirectly harmed by community members who allowed the harm to happen; participated in denial, minimization or victim blaming; or otherwise contributed to harm.

5. **Focus on accountability, not micro-managing someone's life.** If you find yourself or other involved people starting to list out all of the things you do not approve of or cannot stand or want to look different, find a way to step back from being self-righteous, remember humility, and refocus on intervention goals.

6. **Imperfect behavior by the survivor does not excuse violence.** It is common that the survivor of violence acts aggressively, seems manipulative, or does not appear like a completely "innocent victim." See Basics Everyone Should Know, starting on page 17.

7. **Beware of calls for accountability as a way to avoid direct communication.** As community accountability or transformative justice becomes more familiar, it may be tempting to ask for a process of accountability in situations where direct communication may be a more appropriate action. Is this a conflict that could possibly be resolved with mediation or supported conversations?

8. **Figure out the level of engage-ability.** How likely is it that you can make a positive and effective connection with the person who caused harm? Factors related to engage-ability challenges (but not impossibilities) include:
   a. Person has no or very few friends or social connections.
   b. Person experiences issues related to substance abuse and/or mental illness that make accountability difficult.
   c. Person's social connections all collude with or support violent behavior and non-accountability.
   d. Person disengages with (or threatens/harms) anybody who challenges them.
   e. Person is ONLY connected with the survivor.

9. **Be thoughtful about finding the best people to engage with the person who caused harm to take accountability.** Who do they or can they respect? Who can they connect to? Who can stay connected even if bringing up difficult conversations? Who might be less vulnerable to the dynamics of the person who caused harm?

10. **Expect that people often resist accountability**. Most of us struggle with accountability and experience it as a rejection, a threat, and an unjust imposition. We need to create responses that take this struggle into account.

11. **It is okay to remind someone of community consequences to using violence.** Community-based interventions, community accountability, and transformative justice are NOT about excusing violence or coddling those who use violence. They are a way to take violence and its consequences very seriously. Social, personal, or community consequences of using violence are not the same as a threat or the use of punishment. People cannot take responsibility for their violence and make new choices if they are protected from the consequences of their own behavior. Help them make the connection that they risk losing others' respect, compassion, trust, favors, relationships, friendships; their job; etc. when they hurt people with violence. When a person's violence causes them to lose something, it is important not to protect them from ever having to feel regret, sadness, fear, loss, or shame. Again, these are not necessarily punishments and may be the possible human costs for causing harm and suffering.

12. **Stay specific, then give it time.** It is important to make every effort to stay specific, focus on behaviors that we want to address and behaviors that we want to see in the future. Just telling someone to stop being abusive may not give any tools for someone to understand exactly what behaviors were seen as abusive. Focus on specifics.

CREATIVE INTERVENTIONS WORKBOOK

Pathway of Change or Accountability

We use this pathway to show steps toward accountability as a vision of positive and transformative change.

Vision for accountability	Process of change
• Transformational change is possible even for those who commit the most serious acts of violence. • Responsibility over punishment. • Individuals and communities are responsible for change. • Accountability is a process of change. • Any step toward ending or reducing violence can contribute to a bigger vision of community well-being and liberation.	• Each situation calls for distinct actions and changes. • Change may come one step at a time. Each step is significant. • We may not be able to see each step clearly at the outset. • We might work on more than one step at a time, or move from one step to another and back again. • We can aim for the top, but we may not be able to reach it.

TAKING ACCOUNTABILITY

TAKING ACCOUNTABILITY

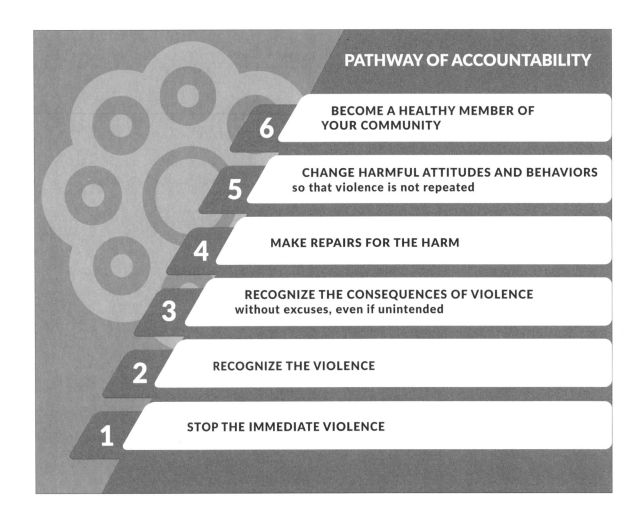

PATHWAY OF ACCOUNTABILITY

6 BECOME A HEALTHY MEMBER OF YOUR COMMUNITY

5 CHANGE HARMFUL ATTITUDES AND BEHAVIORS
so that violence is not repeated

4 MAKE REPAIRS FOR THE HARM

3 RECOGNIZE THE CONSEQUENCES OF VIOLENCE
without excuses, even if unintended

2 RECOGNIZE THE VIOLENCE

1 STOP THE IMMEDIATE VIOLENCE

CREATIVE INTERVENTIONS WORKBOOK

Worksheet:
PATHWAY OF CHANGE OR ACCOUNTABILITY

Use your own words to describe your steps to change or accountability. We placed Step 1 at the bottom – leading up to Step 6 at the top. You can change the order if it is easier for you to go in the other direction.

Step 6 **Become a healthy member of your community**	
Step 5 **Change harmful attitudes/ behaviors**	
Step 4 **Make repairs for the harm**	
Step 3 **Recognize the consequences**	
Step 2 **Recognize the violence**	
Step 1 **Stop the immediate violence**	

Worksheet:

SURVIVOR PARTICIPATION IN TAKING ACCOUNTABILITY

TAKING ACCOUNTABILITY

Survivors can choose how to be involved in a process of taking accountability. This requires special consideration because it can involve some level of connection to the person doing harm. You might have a clear view of what you want from your Goal Setting process (Section D), but things can change as you go. Use this worksheet to think through your desired level of participation in the process.

Component	Considerations	Level of Participation*
Leading or directing	• How much do you want to be leading or directing the process? • How much do you want to set the terms? • How much do you want to work with your allies to set the terms?	
Engagement with the person who caused harm	• What level of initiation do you expect from the person who caused harm and their allies? • How much do you want your input to be prioritized with the process of accountability of the person doing harm?	
Physical presence	• Do you want to be in person at any stage of engaging the person doing harm? • Is there a particular time or way in which you would benefit from being in person? • What is important in terms of your own safety – physical, emotional, other?	
Information & communication	• What kinds of information and communication do you expect or want? • Do you want to weigh in on decisions? • Would you prefer to know a lot, some, or very little?	

*Participation may be very high, high, moderate, low, minimal, or none. For a helpful chart on participation, see the *CI Toolkit*, section 4F, "Taking Accountability Tool F2."

CREATIVE INTERVENTIONS WORKBOOK

Self-Reflection Questions for Survivors & Allies in Taking Accountability

Taking accountability can be a long and difficult process with anticipated resistance from the person doing harm. For the survivor or victim, there is risk of re-living the dynamics of abuse and violence that led to the intervention. These guiding questions can help you and your allies prepare. If you do not feel prepared enough or do not have enough support, then you might reconsider this arena of intervention. However, even asking yourself these questions can be a powerful step toward gaining a sense of power and control. **We recommend starting with "My Wants, My Goals" in Section D.**

1. How are any steps on the "Pathway to Change" in this section above linked to your goals?

2. What do you think could bring about change in the person doing harm?

3. What does the person doing harm care about? This could be things like caring for other people or caring about their reputation or how they're perceived. Anything could count but the strategies would need to change depending upon what these are.

4. Have you seen their potential for change?

    a. If so, could these moments – such as apologies or remorse – be part of a cycle that includes a return to violence?

    b. Are these moments a tool to get what this person wants, such as a return to the relationships, control over the situation, or sympathy?

5. Even if things they care about are self-centered, are they things that could help you reach your goals? If so, what kinds of strategies could use these points as anchors or leverage for you to reach your goals?

6. Is there anything that the person doing harm could say or do that can jeopardize your credibility or your side of the story?

    a. Is there important information that you have not shared with others in the intervention – things that the person doing harm could share?

    b. Can you anticipate the accusations that the person doing harm could make against you? Are you ready to handle these?

7. Is there anything that someone else, including allies or potential allies, could say or do that can jeopardize your credibility?

8. What can be the worst result(s) of this request for accountability?

9. How can you protect yourself from the worst results?

10. Can you live with the worst results?

Worksheet:
SELF-REFLECTION QUESTIONS & PRACTICE FOR ALLIES

Being an ally that supports the process of taking accountability can be challenging. This section includes self-reflection tools for allies. The questions can also be useful for survivors or anyone addressing a situation of harm.

How can I deal with my discomfort with conflict?

What might come up for me in this process (including personal experiences of harm or abuse, my relationship with the person taking accountability, etc.)?

What resources do I have if these things do come up?

How can I separate compassion from collusion or making excuses?

What will I do if I get frustrated, disillusioned, or angry with the person who caused harm in the process? How can I be both true to my feelings and my values? Who can help me be accountable to my values through this process?

Practice: What do I say to the person who caused harm?
(See Home Alive's resource on boundary setting for support: www.teachhomealive. org/curriculum.)

- I care about you.
- I am not rejecting you.
- I want you to have good relationships in your life.
- I want to understand how you are feeling.
- I want to understand what this is like for you.
- I want to support you to change your violence.
- I want to support you to try new responses that might work better.
- How are you doing?
- I think you are blaming the process right now so that you don't have to talk about what's really hard. Is it possible that's true?
- I don't think this kind of violence is ever acceptable. How could you express what is important to you in a nonviolent way?
- I know it can be hard to say what is really going on for you.
- Please lower your voice.
- Do you need to take a break?
- I'm sorry this is so hard.
- I'm sure things can get better, even though they're hard now.
- What might that be like for_____ (other person)?
- Why do you want to make a different choice next time?
- What are you scared of losing?
- I hear you focusing on the other person and their faults.
- What are you responsible for in this situation?
- How do you want me to share my thoughts and observations with you?
- I need a break.
- I believe (the survivor) – we're not here to minimize, deny, or blame them. We want to work on the things that are in your control. What might those things be?
- What do you think it means that (the survivor) experienced this as so hurtful and harmful, but you didn't think it was serious?
- What is one thing you can do this week that feels like a move in a good direction?
- Let's talk.
- Let's hang out again.

TAKING ACCOUNTABILITY

Worksheet:
SELF-REFLECTION QUESTIONS FOR PEOPLE WHO HAVE CAUSED HARM

If you are the person who has caused harm, this worksheet can help guide you to think about accountability. You may want to do this throughout the process to see how your thinking has changed over time.

What harm have I caused – and to whom?

CREATIVE INTERVENTIONS WORKBOOK

Where do these harms come from? Where have I learned them?

What do I understand about how and when I behave in these harmful ways? Are there patterns that show up when I have harmed people and need support? Are there other ways to notice and address these patterns before they lead to causing harm?

TAKING ACCOUNTABILITY

How does my behavior align with my values and my view of who I am or want to be?

TAKING ACCOUNTABILITY

What do I understand about how and when I behave that reflects my best self? When am I my best self? Under what conditions am I or have I been my best self?

Worksheet:
MY ACCOUNTABILITY STATEMENT

If you are taking accountability, you can use this worksheet to reflect on elements that might be important in an accountability statement. Take time to reflect and write. Share with your own accountability group to get constructive feedback. Do not do this in a hurry. Be reflective, be real, be vulnerable, be accountable.

I hear and understand what you have said that I have done. What I've heard is that I have done these harms:

I understand that my attitudes and actions have hurt these people in these ways:

I hear and understand your requests. Your requests are:

I am planning (or already have done or am doing) these actions in order to try to repair these harms:

I am doing the following things or taking the following actions to make sure that I do not repeat these harms in the future:

TAKING
ACCOUNTABILITY

This is my plan for letting others know how I am progressing. I will let others know about my progress in these ways, to these people, at these times, in these ways (e.g., in person meeting, phone call, etc.)

To be clear, my timeline for taking these actions are these:

I would also like to say the following in order to take responsibility for my harm and to do the right thing (name the people or groups who you are addressing):

TAKING
ACCOUNTABILITY

G. WORKING TOGETHER

Working together rests on the belief that interpersonal violence is not just an individual problem but is a community problem requiring a community-level solution. For some of us, the community we bring together might be small – perhaps just a couple of people. For others, a community may be much larger. Whatever the size, working together consists of finding a good group, agreeing on goals, making group decisions, communicating well, and keeping regular check-ins to make sure that everyone is taking action in cooperation with others.

The Importance of Working Together

This entire workbook emphasizes strategies for working together to respond to violence. This section attempts to help correct tendencies to do nothing, rely on others to do more of the work without a group agreement, or to just do one's own thing without regard for the bigger picture. It also calls on us to be compassionate and patient with ourselves and others while doing the difficult work of transforming violence.

Working together increases support for those most affected by the violence, increases support for those involved with the intervention, and counteracts the ways that violence can divide and hurt people. By building a group, we can include more people with a broader range of skills and resources, as well as wisdom and knowledge about the situation and opportunities for change. A collective approach also reduces isolation, provides more leverage in taking accountability, and closes gaps for people to slip out of responsibility. Ideally, working together strengthens relationships of care and concern for the survivor, person doing harm, and others. It can build a community or collective with skills and practices that might prevent violence in the future.

KEY QUESTIONS
1. Who can work together? 2. What are their roles? 3. Does everyone know and agree with the goals and roles? 4. How will you communicate and coordinate? 5. How will you make decisions?

Tips for Working Together

Take the time to meet in person	Most people are not taught how to respond to violence, and there are few common understandings about how to do this well. It is useful to find out people's unique priorities, concerns, and bottom-lines. Building group trust and relationships takes time.
Stay in communication with the person doing harm	Because people are often uncomfortable dealing with the person doing harm, that person can be kept out of the loop. They can begin to build up anxiety if there is no communication or if communication is vague and impersonal. You may need to choose someone whose role is to keep the person doing harm informed.
Expect differences, take them seriously, and work to find common ground	Reactions to violence are often emotional, and responses can be very different. Even when people agree on what happened and who is responsible, they often differ on what should be done and how to get there. If a group does not recognize and work through differences to a common decision, they can cause mistakes that are not only frustrating, but potentially dangerous. Use the "Our Values" worksheet on page 37 to help your group get clearer on your shared values.
Working together may require major compromises	This could mean deciding what is most important to move toward a ground goal. It is rare for everyone to feel 100 percent good about an intervention. People working together must decide whether they can live with the compromises.
Not everyone can be a good team player	Make use of the "Mapping Allies and Barriers" section to determine who might be a good team member. You may find allies where you would least expect it. You may also identify people who you do not want on your team. People may also join at first and find that they cannot agree enough to stay involved.
Build care, fun, and sustainability into the process of working together	These can be little things, such as: checking in with how people are doing at the start and end of each meeting, making room for spiritual practices that are meaningful for the group, sharing meals, guarding against overwhelming feelings of bitterness or disappointment, recalling larger goals and values, bringing humor to the mistakes that will be made along the way, noticing when people are burning out or have personal issues they must attend to, and celebrating achievements large and small.

WORKING TOGETHER

Checklist:
TEAM ROLES

Use this tool to help match team roles with the people who could play that role well. Think about whether someone is already playing this role, if they are right for the role, and/or if someone needs to be recruited to play this role. Note that some people can play multiple roles. You do not need a different person for each role or every role to be filled to carry out your intervention.

Role	Description/Qualities	Name(s)
Facilitator or Anchor The one who holds the process.	The facilitator is a key role. A good person for this role is trusted; level-headed; not too involved in the situation of violence, but knowledgeable; able to see the big picture; able to move things along; a good communicator; and has a good memory or way of recording.	
Coordinator The glue.	The coordinator makes sure that everyone on the team is on board with decisions, working well together, getting the right information. A good person for this role is trusted, able to see the big picture, sensitive to others, good at being inclusive and not leaving people out, good working with different personalities. This can be a role taken on by the facilitator or anchor.	
Logistics Deals with the details of time and place.	This is a person who makes sure there's a place to meet; there are food and drinks at the meeting; access needs are acknowledged and met – or gaps are communicated; there's paper, tissues, and other supplies as needed. A good person for this role is responsible, detail-oriented, and organized.	

WORKING TOGETHER

Role	Description/Qualities	Name(s)
Notetaker Keeps the details.	This is a person who takes notes or uses other ways to keep track of basic information about what has happened; goals; safety plan; communications received by the survivor, person doing harm, and others; and steps taken. A good person for this role is detail-oriented, has a good memory, and is able to keep notes in an organized and safe place.	
Nurturer Keeps people feeling good.	This is a person that keeps people in a caring, compassionate environment. A good person for this role is trusted, caring, and compassionate.	
Reality Checker Makes sure we are doing things that are realistic.	This person thinks about what is likely to happen and tries to prevent unrealistic expectations that could lead to frustration or burn out. A good person for this role has a good understanding of the people and situation, can bring people back without losing sight of goals, gets real without negativity.	
Communicator Makes sure we are listening to each other, checking in, following up.	This role is similar to the Coordinator, but the focus is on communication – verbal, written, etc. The Communicator makes sure people share the right information within a reasonable amount of time and have good follow up. A good person for this role is trusted, understands that different people give and receive information differently, has good follow up.	
Vision-keeper Helps us keep our vision.	This person keeps an eye to loftier goals and reminds people when morale sinks or when people begin to be driven by hate or revenge. A good person for this role is visionary, has high ideals, and is a good communicator.	

WORKING TOGETHER

Tools and Worksheets

Role	Description/Qualities	Name(s)
Cheerleader Keeps people energized and positive.	This person helps keep a positive team spirit. A good person for this role is enthusiastic, inspirational, and/or fun.	
Supporter Supports, stands by, and advocates for the key people.	All groups need people who are able to act to support the survivor, other vulnerable people such as children, the person doing harm, an organization that may be suffering under the weight of violence, or others that may have a particularly stressful or difficult role. Supporters look out for their needs and help advocate when others are not paying enough attention. A good person for this role is trusted, compassionate, able to balance the needs of one person with those of the group.	
Add another role:	All situations are different, Use the space below to add any additional roles that are important to your group.	

CREATIVE INTERVENTIONS WORKBOOK

Worksheet:
AGREEMENTS FOR SUSTAINING OVER TIME

Keeping teams together is difficult work. These are some basic agreements that others have used that may be helpful.

1. Check in to see what everyone is thinking and feeling about the situation you are working on – make room for confusion, doubts, and questioning.
2. When in doubt, ask a question.
3. Take notes or use whatever method works for you and your group to keep a record (photos of notes, video clips, etc.) – you won't remember and things get more confusing over time (you may want to assign a Notetaker).
4. Review and clarify decisions – make sure you all agree on what you decided.
5. Praise efforts and celebrate achievements – celebrating even the small things can take you a long way.
6. When someone is absent, follow up with them to see what happened, if they are okay, and to let them know you expect accountability.
7. Forgive each other, cut each other slack, and, at the same time, find a way to get necessary steps done.
8. Make sure steps and goals match the team's capacity or what's possible.
9. Make criticisms specific and constructive.
10. Move toward resolution. Move away from gossip.

Add your own agreements here:

WORKING TOGETHER

H. KEEPING ON TRACK

A process of violence intervention is likely to be made up of many moments when decisions need to be made, actions are taken, and next steps are planned and reviewed. Keeping on track makes sure that the overall intervention is going well, that goals are in place, and that the process is moving forward in a good direction. It includes self-checks for groups and for individuals to make sure that everyone is moving toward the goals. It gives opportunities for adjustments to be made as actions are taken along the way and situations change.

Closure is also an important aspect to keeping on track. See the final page on closure as an important part of any intervention.

KEY QUESTIONS
1. Are we ready to take the next step?
2. How did it go?
3. What did we achieve?
4. Did we celebrate our achievements (even the small ones)?
5. What needs to change?
6. What is the next step?

Worksheet:
HOW ARE WE DOING? GROUP GUIDING QUESTIONS

These are general questions to ask along the way to help make sure things are working smoothly:

1. Do we have clear goals and bottom lines still? What are they?

2. Are we guided by clear values? What are they?

3. Do we all seem to be on the same page? If not, who is on the same page? Who is not? What can we do to get everyone on the same page?

4. Are we working through disagreements or conflicts in a good way?

5. Are we getting enough support?

6. Are we offering enough support?

7. Are we keeping connected to and supporting the survivor?

8. Are we keeping connected to and supporting the person doing harm?

9. Are we taking care of people who are vulnerable or need our extra care (for example children, elders, chronically ill and disabled people, etc.)?

10. Are we regularly doing risk assessment and safety planning?

11. Are we moving forward, or do we have a clear action plan with the right people taking responsibility for each piece? Do we have specific tasks or expectations and reasonable timelines?

12. Are we flexible enough to consider new opportunities or unanticipated road-blocks?

13. Are there things we need to change? What are they?

14. Do we have a good system or plan for change? If not, what changes need to be made?

15. What are the next steps?

KEEPING ON TRACK

Closure

When to close an intervention can be a challenging question. We encourage you to build your thoughts and expectations about closure closer to the beginning as you set your goals and determine the best processes to meet those goals.

Things to think about regarding closure are:

- Goals and what you can expect to meet given your anticipated process. Some goals, for example, healing (which may or may not be one of your goals) – may be ones you want to address from your intervention but may also be an ongoing goal met through other parts of your life – and beyond the length of this intervention.

- Time, energy, and availability of people who are key to holding the intervention or process for a longer term. Not everyone may be necessary for a successful longer-term intervention, but some key people will be. Can they be around for the long term? Can you think of ways to sustain each other?

- Realistic timelines for goals to be reached. Everyone wants transformation to happen immediately, but this is not usually the case. Long-term processes of engagement to support someone who has caused harm may go on for a year to eighteen months (for example, see Support New York at supportny.org). How can you divide roles and responsibilities so that the right people are there for the right support – but not everyone has to be there for everything? The facilitator/anchor and coordinator(s) can be key in thinking through the rhythm and roles of an intervention.

- Processes can be bridges toward longer-term transformations. The intervention/process/circle may offer a way to get clear on harms, consider safety, determine realistic goals, and figure out supportive ways to reach those goals – but may not take you all the way to the end. Think about generating momentum and handing off people involved to other resources to reach those goals. If you are approaching an intervention as a bridge, think of ways to report back progress at intervals up to a certain time period. Think through format and chain of communication.

- A group or team may also consider closure when progress is not being made, but everyone decides that you have done the best you can.

- In any case – whether closure comes at the end of success or due to a period of challenge and seeming failure – we encourage you to celebrate whatever successes you have reached. For Creative Interventions, we have come to recognize ebb and flow as the nature of transformation and change.

Worksheet:
OUR PLAN FOR CLOSURE

This is a worksheet to come up with your group plan for closure.

This is our plan for closure. We expect to close if/when these goals are reached. Include expected timeline. Think about how you will know that goal is reached (in a good-enough way) and plan for reporting back (what format and communication chain).

ADDITIONAL
RESOURCES

ADDITIONAL RESOURCES

Below is a selection of resources on transformative justice, processes, and abolition, part of a growing collection of toolkits, webinars, articles, and other resources on transformative justice. This list primarily relies upon free (or very low-cost) materials.

CREATIVE INTERVENTIONS

Creative Interventions

Website includes free downloadable English and Spanish PDF version of the *Creative Interventions Toolkit.*

creative-interventions.org

Storytelling & Organizing Project

Website includes stories about everyday people taking action to end interpersonal violence. Audio and transcripts available for free download.

stopviolenceeveryday.org

SOME ARTICLES ON TRANSFORMATIVE JUSTICE

Alisa Bierria, Clarissa Rojas Durazo, and Mimi Kim, "Community Accountability: Emerging Movements to Transform Violence," special issue of *Social Justice Journal* (Vol. 37, no. 4, 2011–2012).

Mimi Kim, "From Carceral Feminism to Transformative Justice: Women of Color Feminism and Alternatives to Incarceration," *Journal of Ethnic & Cultural Diversity in Social Work* 27, no. 1 (May 2018): 1–15.

transformharm.org/wp-content/uploads/2018/12/Kim-2018-FromCarceralFeminismtoTransformativeJustice.pdf

Mia Mingus, "Transformative Justice: A Brief Description," *Leaving Evidence* (blog), January 9, 2019.

leavingevidence.wordpress.com/2019/01/09/transformative-justice-a-brief-description

OTHER GENERAL COMMUNITY ACCOUNTABILITY AND TRANSFORMATIVE JUSTICE RESOURCES

(Note: not all are active now, but their websites still have resources available for the public.)

Barnard Center for Research on Women: Building Accountable Communities

A resource hub for videos, webinars and other resources on transformative justice.

bcrw.barnard.edu/building-accountable-communities

Bay Area Transformative Justice Collective

Includes a curriculum for transformative justice study and pod-mapping resources.

batjc.wordpress.com

Generation FIVE: *Transformative Justice Handbook*

Free download of their *Ending Child Sexual Abuse: A Transformative Justice Handbook.*

generationfive.org

Just Practice

A collective supporting trainings/coaching on harm reduction & transformative justice.

just-practice.org

Just Practice Mixtape Series

Steps to End Prisons and Policing: A Mixtape Series offers important and useful videos on various aspects of transformative justice.

just-practice.org/steps-to-end-prisons-policing-a-mix-tape-on-transformative-justice

Philly Stands Up

A collective working in Philadelphia to confront sexual assault using a transformative justice framework.

phillystandsup.wordpress.com

Project Nia

A grassroots organization that works to end the arrest, detention, and incarceration of children/young adults by promoting restorative and transformative justice practices.

project-nia.org

Spring Up
Youth and young adult serving collective working to prevent and respond to gender-based violence with consent education and transformative justice.

timetospringup.org

Support New York
A collective supporting transformative justice processes addressing sexual violence. Website offers resources sharing their processes and lessons learned.

supportny.org

Transform Harm
A comprehensive resource hub about ending violence. Includes an introduction to transformative justice, and articles, audio-visual materials, curricula, and more.

transformharm.org

Transformative Justice Project of Brown University
Resources list and links to TJ-related documents.

docs.google.com/document/d/1MCnYZEc4075DH9ZDyoDBfeZDBtqkV3q7gy_t1wLwRkc/edit

Vision Change Win
A team of social justice consultants who have developed resources addressing transformative justice and community safety. See their toolkit, *Get In Formation: A Community Safety Toolkit.*

visionchangewin.com

ADDITIONAL RESOURCES ON PROCESSES & CIRCLES

Home Alive
A useful curriculum on boundary setting in threatening situations.

teachhomealive.org/curriculum

Mariame Kaba and Shira Hassan, *Fumbling Towards Repair: A Workbook for Community Accountability Facilitators* (Chicago: Project Nia, 2019).
A very useful workbook intended to follow the content of the *Creative Interventions Toolkit* – specifically written for those facilitating processes.

Little Books of Restorative Justice
A book series published by Simon and Schuster
simonandschuster.com

Living Justice Press
A nonprofit publisher for restorative justice
livingjusticepress.org

Jovida Ross and Weyam Ghadbian, *Turning Towards Each Other: A Conflict Workbook*
A useful free workbook on interpersonal and group conflict.
**96cd8e90-7f87-4399-af6b-c7156e91189a.filesusr.com/ugd/05f4b7_
cec53ab03dcd4f32b1fecaf66ede2d80.pdf**

RESOURCES SPECIFICALLY RELATED TO ACCOUNTABILITY

Joe Biel and Faith G. Harper, *How to be Accountable Workbook: Take Responsibility to Change Your Behavior* (Portland, OR: Microcosm Publishing, 2020).

Mia Mingus, "The Four Parts of Accountability: How to Give a Genuine Apology," *Leaving Evidence* (blog), December 18, 2019.
leavingevidence.wordpress.com/2019/12/18/how-to-give-a-good-apology-part-1-the-four-parts-of-accountability

PATRIARCHY/TOXIC MASCULINITY

(Thanks to Dara Bayer, Xochi Carland, and Camila Pelsinger of Brown University's Transformative Justice Project for this list. See full list of Brown's TJ resources cited above.)

Paul Brown, *Don't Be a Dick* (Self-published zine: n.d.).
supportnewyork.files.wordpress.com/2018/04/dontbeadick.pdf.

Barry Deutsch, "Male Privilege Checklist," *Alas, a Blog* (defunct blog).
www.csueastbay.edu/dsj/files/docs/popular-media/dsjguide-male-privilege.pdf.

Leah Lakshmi Piepzna-Samarasinha, "A Modest Proposal for a Fair Trade Emotional Labor Economy (Centered by Disabled, Femme of Color, Working-Class/Poor Genius)" in *Care Work: Dreaming Disability Justice* (Vancouver: Arsenal Pulp Press, 2018, pp.136-148.

The Challenging Male Supremacy Project, "What Does It Feel Like When Change Finally Comes: Male Supremacy, Accountability, and Transformative Justice," in *The Revolution Starts at Home: Confronting Intimate Violence within Activist Communities*, eds., Ching-In Chen, Jai Dulani, and Leah Lakshmi Piepzna-Samarasinha (Chico, CA: AK Press, 2016).

The Chrysalis Collective, "Beautiful, Difficult, Powerful: Ending Sexual Assault Through Transformative Justice," in *The Revolution Starts at Home: Confronting Intimate Violence within Activist Communities*, eds., Ching-In Chen, Jai Dulani, and Leah Lakshmi Piepzna-Samarasinha (Chico, CA: AK Press, 2016).

"Cis Privilege Checklist," on the blog *Taking Up Too Much Space: Trans Misogyny, Feminism, and Trans Activism*.
takesupspace.wordpress.com/cis-privilege-checklist

Terrence Crowley, "The Lie of Entitlement," in *Transforming A Rape Culture*, eds. Emilie Buchwald, Pamela R. Fletcher, and Martha Roth (Minneapolis: Milkweed Editions, 1993).

bell hooks, *Understanding Patriarchy* (Louisville, KY: Louisville Anarchist Federation, 2010).
imaginenoborders.org/pdf/zines/UnderstandingPatriarchy.pdf

Robert Jensen, "Rape, Rape Culture, and the Problem of Patriarchy," *Waging Nonviolence*, April 29, 2014.
wagingnonviolence.org/2014/04/rape-rape-culture-problem-patriarchy

Jackson Katz, "Violence Against Women – It's a Men's Issue," *TEDtalk* (video), November 2012
ted.com/talks/jackson_katz_violence_against_women_it_s_a_men_s_issue

Richard S. Orton, "Learning to Listen: One Man's Work in the Antirape Movement," in *Transforming A Rape Culture*, eds. Emilie Buchwald, Pamela R. Fletcher, and Martha Roth (Minneapolis: Milkweed Editions, 1993).

Nora Samaran, "Dating Tips for the Feminist Man," *norasamaran.com* (blog), February 11, 2016.

norasamaran.com/2016/02/11/dating-tips-for-the-feminist-man.

Nora Samaran, "The Opposite of Rape Culture is Nurturance Culture," *norasamaran.com* (blog), February 11, 2016.

https://norasamaran.com/2016/02/11/the-opposite-of-rape-culture-is-nurturance-culture-2

RESOURCES ON ABOLITION

The Abolition and Disability Justice Coalition
Principles and tools for abolition based upon disability justice.
abolitionanddisabilityjustice.com

Critical Resistance
The abolitionist organization has developed a resource hub on abolition.
criticalresistance.org

Project Nia
"Building your Abolitionist Toolkit: Everyday Resources for a Punishment-Free World."
https://project-nia.org/news/building-your-abolitionist-toolkit-everyday-resources-for-a-punishment-free-world

This Workbook is a companion to the
Creative Interventions Toolkit, **also available:**

"The *Creative Interventions Toolkit* is my go-to reference whenever I begin a new community accountability intervention. I've often remarked that it is the Bible for most facilitators I know." – Mariame Kaba

Pick up a copy at **akpress.org** or your favorite bookstore!
Also available online at **creative-interventions.org**

AK PRESS is small, in terms of staff and resources, but we also manage to be one of the world's most productive anarchist publishing houses. We publish close to twenty books every year, and distribute thousands of other titles published by like-minded independent presses and projects from around the globe. We're entirely worker run and democratically managed. We operate without a corporate structure—no boss, no managers, no bullshit.

The **FRIENDS OF AK PRESS** program is a way you can directly contribute to the continued existence of AK Press, and ensure that we're able to keep publishing books like this one! Friends pay $25 a month directly into our publishing account ($30 for Canada, $35 for international), and receive a copy of every book AK Press publishes for the duration of their membership! Friends also receive a discount on anything they order from our website or buy at a table: 50% on AK titles, and 30% on everything else. We have a Friends of AK ebook program as well: $15 a month gets you an electronic copy of every book we publish for the duration of your membership. *You can even sponsor a very discounted membership for someone in prison.*

Email **friendsofak@akpress.org** for more info, or visit the website: **https://www.akpress.org/friends.html**.

There are always great book projects in the works—so sign up now to become a Friend of AK Press, and let the presses roll!